NURSING
AT THE FRONTLINE
A WW2 DIARY FROM NORTH AFRICA AND ITALY

GRAHAM BANDY

Pen & Sword
MILITARY
AN IMPRINT OF PEN & SWORD BOOKS LTD.
YORKSHIRE · PHILADELPHIA

First published in Great Britain in 2024 by
Pen & Sword Military
An imprint of
Pen & Sword Books Ltd
Yorkshire - Philadelphia

Copyright © Graham Bandy, 2024

ISBN 978 1 39908 842 8

The right of Graham Bandy to be identified as the Author of this work has been asserted by him in accordance with the Copyright, Designs and Patents Act 1988.

A CIP catalogue record for this book is available from the British Library.

All rights reserved. No part of this book may be reproduced or transmitted in any form or by any means, electronic or mechanical, including photocopying, recording or by any information storage and retrieval system, without permission from the Publisher in writing.

Typeset by SJmagic DESIGN SERVICES, India.

Printed and bound in the UK by CPI Group (UK) Ltd.

Pen & Sword Books Limited incorporates the imprints of Archaeology, Atlas, Aviation, Battleground, Digital, Discovery, Family History, Fiction, History, Local, Local History, Maritime, Military, Military Classics, Politics, Select, Transport, True Crime, After the Battle, Air World, Claymore Press, Frontline Publishing, Leo Cooper, Remember When, Seaforth Publishing, The Praetorian Press, Wharncliffe Books, Wharncliffe Local History, Wharncliffe Transport, Wharncliffe True Crime and White Owl.

For a complete list of Pen & Sword titles please contact

PEN & SWORD BOOKS LIMITED
George House, Units 12 & 13, Beevor Street, Off Pontefract Road,
Barnsley, South Yorkshire, S71 1HN, England
E-mail: enquiries@pen-and-sword.co.uk
Website: www.pen-and-sword.co.uk

or

PEN AND SWORD BOOKS
1950 Lawrence Rd, Havertown, PA 19083, USA
E-mail: uspen-and-sword@casematepublishers.com
Website: www.penandswordbooks.com

Contents

Introduction vii
Acknowledgements ix
Who was Harold/Harry/'Scra'? x
Preface xii

Did I Choose Wisely? 1
The Oral Examination 2
On to Algeria and Tunis 5
An Interesting Souvenir 10
Carthage 12
The Convent Hospital 16
By George! 21
Digging for Pleasure 24
Medical Duty 37
Hammamet 44
Kairouan 48
The Jerboa 57
The Return to Carthage, and our First Christmas away from Home ... 59
On to Italy 71
Bari 78
Background to Bari, Partisans and the SOE Mission to Yugoslavia 86

Reception of Partisan Refugees at Bari 89
Priority Babies 104
73 (Spitfire) Squadron, Cannae, Italy 106
Winter 1944/1945, 73 Squadron 124
A Winter's Tale 129
Interlude: Ablution Supreme 133
The Squadron Farewell and on to Yugoslavia 135
Brindisi 161
Rome 163
Malta 171
Home at Last 176

Further Reading and Bibliography 179
Index 181

Introduction

About ten years ago I attended an event, to display my First and Second World War medical uniforms, badges and large amounts of equipment. It was here that I was approached by an older lady, who asked if I would be interested in a handwritten manuscript that her neighbour had produced about his medical career in the Second World War. I said that of course I would be. She asked if I could pop round to her house the following weekend, which I duly did. I was handed three plastic bags full of notes, folders, photographs and watercolours by an RAF Nursing Orderly called 'LAC Scrafield, H'.

She handed the bags over, on the proviso that I get the manuscript published for its author. He and his wife had died some years before, without issue or known relatives, and she informed me that she had been waiting for 'the right sort of person' to come along. Apparently, I was it!

During the next few years, work and several house moves got in the way, until a year or so ago, I found myself living in Sussex, not a million miles from 'Scra's' home, and with time on my hands to go through the numerous unopened boxes which had followed me around, or sat in storage, for all those years.

I had forgotten what a treasure trove of notes, photos and watercolours there was in these now disintegrating bags. I carefully sorted the many loose papers out and put the pictures into archival folders.

I had just sent my first book to Pen & Sword, and I thought that my editor, Tara, should see this too. Thus, over forty years since Scra wrote down his memoirs in longhand, almost eighty since the events they describe, and ten since I was entrusted with them, here they are. They do make for a fascinating read. From Carthage and the White Sisters to the events connected to his attachment to the SOE medical mission to Yugoslavia, these memoirs take you deep into the world of the wartime male RAF Nursing Orderly, alongside his duties, escapades and the love of art that carried him through some dark times.

The words you read are his, verbatim. *All my comments, clarifications and notes are in italic script.*

I have changed nothing in this story, simply edited it a little and added some background and colour to the canvas.

These tales are told in a matter-of-fact way that some may find insensitive, but I can assure you, dear reader, that even from my recent sojourns in the forces and also in Nursing, so much of this rings true and resonates with me. It is a story of its time and of its people, written in language which carries the social mores and black humour of the services. As the great comedian Spike Milligan once wrote to a critic of his own published military memoirs, 'If it wasn't for the humour and language (that carried us through), this letter would be coming to you from a grave somewhere in Italy.'

Acknowledgements

First of all, I'd like to thank Liz Graham in South Africa for her relentless search for the records of Lt Duchen. I must also thank Nel Dewald, also of South Africa, for his splendid assistance in finding them.

Thanks are always due to my wife for her help and for upping my Earl Grey allowance when writing, as even she acknowledges, 'Graham works better with tea!'

My thanks to George and Harriet and indeed all at Pen & Sword for having me back again for another tome.

As always, there are many friends and colleagues who also continue to put up with me, particularly those at the Society of Genealogists, who continue to ask me back to give talks and lectures on their behalf. Sadly, I've not the room to mention everyone, but rest assured you are in my thoughts, and you may well be reading this in a complimentary copy!!

Who was Harold/Harry/'Scra'?

Harold Scrafield was born on 19 March 1903 to William Edward and Sarah Scrafield. Harry's father was an Assistant Superintendent Class II for the General Post Office.

He was the youngest of eight children, and by 1921, when he was eighteen, both his parents had died and he was living at 45 Mildmay Grove, near Mildmay Park, between Highbury and Stoke Newington in London. He was sharing with some of his siblings, and the head of the house on the census for that year was his brother Ernest, who had also become a postman, like his father.

Harry, however, was destined for other things and had begun working at R. Hovender and Sons of 89–95 City Road in London. They were very well known as wholesale perfumiers, wholesale sundriesmen, wig makers and hairdressing sundriesmen! Harry was with them until he joined up in 1942.

Harry married Edith Irene Mabel Hutton, but for some reason she eschewed those Christian names and became known as Marjorie Scrafield. Interestingly, her burial record for 17 July 1981 names her as 'Marjorie Scrafield, otherwise Edith Irene Mabel Scrafield'. I have never seen such an entry before on a civilian grave. It is common on the Commonwealth War Graves to see 'Served as . . .' etc., but this form of entry I have not seen.

Her father and mother were Herbert, a carpenter originally from Plumstead, and Ada (née Steel) from Limehouse in London.

Interestingly, the 1901 census places her at 'Mabel Villa, Maybury Road' in Woking aged eleven months. In 1911, she can be found at 7 Wilfred Street, Woking (which is off Mabel Road!); by then she also had two sisters, Enid and Dorothy.

In 1919 she appears on the electoral roll on Wandsworth High Street, and on the 1921 census, she is with her family in Wandsworth. Her father was by then a General Foreman of Works for a builders' firm, and Edith/Marjorie was a clerk with the Ministry of Pensions in Regents Park.

She met and then married Harold in May 1926, and by 1939 he was a Departmental Manager for Hovender's. He was also very active as an ARP Warden.

Oddly, I have found a 1926 birth record for a Marjorie Joan Scrafield, with a mother's maiden name of Hutton. I have found absolutely no other record for her at all!

Going through all the pictures again, I have noted that one is addressed to Joan and signed 'love daddy'; there is also a letter to them in the file sending 'best wishes to you both and Joan' in 1978 – but there is little else about her at all. There are three entries in the early 2000s on electoral rolls for Brighton in Sussex and Liss in Hampshire, but that is the sum total of her in the records. A conundrum . . .

It is from here that 'Scra', as he became known, was eventually found for enlistment.

His story follows . . .

Preface

'I remember, I remember, the house where I was born . . .'

So wrote the poet Thomas Hood. Similarly, I can now look back nostalgically to the day when a new life commenced for me. Totally different to that which I had hitherto been accustomed. On 2nd July 1942, at the grand old age of thirty-nine, I was enlisted into the Royal Air Force. Rather late in life to start a new career!

I shall refrain from giving details of my initial training, so abhorred by all recruits, and rather concentrate on aspects of life abroad, and the various countries in which I served.

It is often said, 'Oh, forget the war, it finished years ago.' Up to a point I agree; all the privations and horrors are best forgotten, and indeed nature has been kind here. It is strange, but happy memories seem to remain vivid, whilst sad and unhappy incidents fade in the mind. To me, the mention of the war brings to mind long and hazardous journeys through North Africa, Sicily, Italy, Yugoslavia, Malta and finally the length of France to return home. And so, I trust that the incidents I shall relate (interesting, I hope, and sometimes amusing) and which I experienced as an RAF Medic will remind some of my readers (and inform those who were not there) of the happier side of what we may perhaps, refer to as 'Enforced Labour'.

During my service I was offered promotion twice, to serve in Medical Statistics – in a record office. Both of these proposals I politely refused. I was, and indeed still am, fascinated with practical nursing, and not dry, mundane office work with no patient contact.

> *This is one of the many areas where Scra and I are of one mind. I never really enjoyed my managerial posts at all, stuck behind a desk.*

PREFACE

I shall try to describe the countries I visited, the medical experience I gained and the comradely relationships which prevailed amongst all ranks. The Service, no matter which branch, remains the great leveller of personalities.

All the stories related here are true . . . if not all enjoyable.

Did I Choose Wisely?

Upon enlistment in the RAF the recruit was offered the choice of becoming a fitter, a radio operator, or even of being a 'Valiant Pilot'. I think that the choice was actually fictitious; one ended up in the trade which needed the personnel at the time. I did not have much choice as I was comparatively old – in fact, the kind, smiling Sergeant greeted me with the words, 'Where the hell have you been hiding for the past two years that the war has been on?!'

I replied that I had been a warden in the London Blitz.

'So, you know First Aid – any certificates?'

I replied that I had.

'Right. Med Branch for you!'

I must admit that I had previously acquired a fair knowledge of First Aid; this was a subject much to my liking. After a period of 'square bashing' I proceeded to the medical school for a twelve-week intensive course. Every applicant appeared before a selection board of three doctors. If accepted, no time was wasted. The applicant was sent straight into a class of around thirty pupils, most of whom were the same age as myself – the 'Old Dads'.

What a crash course! It took three months of intensive study, although the First Aid was kids' stuff to me. Lectures began at 0900 and went on until lunch. We were back again at 1400 until tea at 1700. This was followed by what was called 'silent study' from 1800 to 2000. Sunday was a rest day, which was mainly spent studying the notes taken during the previous week's lectures, with our tender-hearted Sergeant giving us from time to time a little encouragement, such as 'If you don't pass your finals, no seven days leave for you!' These 'finals' consisted of written papers on anatomy, physiology, pathology, hygiene and sanitation, and they were followed by an oral examination by three doctors. In my class, only two failed, which was not bad considering the ages of the pupils.

The Oral Examination

I was the last student to be called by the three doctors for my oral.

'Ah! . . . Now? . . . What can we find for you?' asked the Wing Commander medical officer. 'You may sit down to answer the questions.'

He smiled, trying to reassure me. I settled into the chair, and he began.

'Describe – in detail – the following process. Imagine you have placed a piece of bread into your mouth. Describe, in your own way, the entire process, through the digestive system of the piece of bread, until it reaches the anus.'

Sitting down, I covered my eyes with my hands to visualise the process and to concentrate. I went through all the key words – masticate, bolus, swallow, oesophagus, salivary glands, etc. I was constantly interrupted by all three of them on this complicated subject, but they appeared satisfied.

'Next question . . . If you saw a patient supporting his left elbow, what would be your diagnosis and treatment?'

'A possible fracture of the clavicle', came my instant reply.

There were further questions on the nervous system, and again I managed to satisfy the board.

After the examination, my marks came through – 96 per cent. I had passed, and passed well. My reward came – seven days home leave.

Seven days of happiness at home soon slipped by, and then I was off to a General Hospital for practical training (bed-making, bed pan drill, etc.) under the eagle eye of the 'battle-axe' – Matron. No matter how distasteful the task, one seemed to be toughened, so as to be able to cope confidently with the various duties whenever called upon. This served us in good stead as time and experience went on in the service. It was during this period of 'practical' that I was able to observe for a while

THE ORAL EXAMINATION

The training group at Sidmouth in Devon, end of course picture.

The accommodation for the course. The Royal Glen, now a Grade 1 listed family-run hotel.

the treatment for burns by complete immersion in saline baths. This was most effective and interesting, as it had only been recently discovered that aircrew crashing into the sea after or even whilst burning had a much faster recuperation rate than those who had crashed on land.

On to Algeria and Tunis

After a brief spell at some godforsaken satellite aerodrome in Lincolnshire, where the usual order was heard each morning, 'Fall in the sick, lame and lazy!' (and believe me, this was very apt!), my number came up for a tour overseas. I was to be attached to a newly formed Mobile Field Hospital. Eventually, we sailed in convoy to 'destination unknown' on 10th March 1943.

> *Scra may have misremembered this a little.*
>
> *31 Mobile Field Hospital's personnel were assembled at No.1 Personnel Dispatch Centre West Kirby in Lincolnshire on 22 March 1943. The following three weeks were spent equipping all to a 'tropical scale of issue' (kit and uniform), checking stores and the mechanical transport, familiarizing the new hospital staff with Mobile Field Hospital equipment and sorting out the paper work and orders for convoy orders.*

The only clue we had was the issue of tropical kit.

> *This would have been the lightweight 'khaki drill' uniform made of a light denim material, and 'tropical', i.e. for points east and south of Gibraltar, not the scratchy woollen uniform being worn in Europe!*

The convoy was attacked by an enemy submarine as we passed through the Straits of Gibraltar and two troopships were sunk. It was a very nerve-wracking time.

After ten days at sea we eventually arrived and disembarked at Algiers on 24th April, in spring-like weather, which became hotter with each succeeding day. We stayed for a short time at Maison Carré, a small village on the outskirts of the town.

Instructions were received on May 25th for the MFH to move eastwards by road to Carthage in Tunisia. An advance party was sent out on the 26th and the main party on the 27th. Then, in a road convoy of lorries and ambulances, we commenced our first long journey by road to Tunis via the Atlas Mountains.

> *In fact, Scra celebrated his fortieth birthday at sea, on 19 March. He was indeed one of the oldest newly enlisted LACs in the RAF!*
>
> *Maison Carré is now known as 'El Harrach' and is a suburb of the capital, Algiers. It has a population of 49,000. I don't think Scra would recognise it today!*

This journey was, to me, the most interesting of all. We crawled along very slowly through unknown surroundings, along precipitous, narrow tracks through the foothills, where the ever-changing scenery was

On the way out to Tunisia; convoy off the North African Coast, 1943.

breathtaking. The early mornings were the best; in the crisp, clear air the sunlight caught the snow-capped mountain peaks, colouring them a rich shell-pink and accentuating the deep shadows of the ravines. To complete the picture, there were masses of wild narcissi growing on the mountain slopes like a luxuriant carpet. Their fragrance floated down to us – at a distance of what must have been at least three miles. Every evening towards dusk, a halt was made for a meal and a night's rest. The immense expanse of the rich dark blue of the night sky and the incessant noises of the crickets and bullfrogs soon lulled us to sleep under the shelter of the vehicles.

The journey to Tunis took us four days. We passed through many Arab villages, the principal halts being made at Ben Masour, Setif, Le Khroub and Souk Ahras. In fact, I still have the slip of paper giving the route to be followed. (*It is in fact, a road journey of 560 miles from Algiers to Tunis.*)

Altogether the list contains thirty place names. En route at Madjez-el-Bab we came across burning tanks. We hastily dug graves and marked them with an inverted rifle topped with a 'tin hat'. This 'initiation' brought us back to the grim reality of the tasks ahead.

These burning tanks were the result of the advance of the vanguard of the composite force of the First and Eighth British Armies under Lieutenant General Brian Horrocks, in what proved to be the last battle of the North African campaign. Hannibal, many, many years before, had said that 'Whoever holds Madjez-el-Bab holds the key to the door and is master of all Tunisia.'

This was now the second attempt at taking Tunis. The first had failed in the previous November, after the Germans had counter-attacked.

In January 1943, Rommel had been placed in command of the German Afrika Korps, and on 6 March he launched an attack (Operation Capri) on the Allies at Medenine which failed, with the Germans being forced to retreat. Hitler then rejected Rommel's request to be allowed to withdraw. On 9 March, Rommel left Tunisia on health grounds. It was questioned at the time by Kesselring and

On the way to Tunis through the Atlas Mountains.

other Germans whether the Allies had somehow got hold of inside information. It was not revealed until fairly recently that the capture of Enigma and the breaking of the Ultra code had indeed revealed all the movements of Axis forces, not only in North Africa, but also in Europe and of the Atlantic U-Boat flotillas.

Tunis was finally taken on 7 May 1943, with the 11th Hussars forming the vanguard of the 7th Armoured Division and being the first to enter the city. Between 6 and 13 May, 130,000 Germans and 118,000 Italians, including twenty-two Generals, were captured.

We were now only a few miles from our destination, and we were really on the heels of the First Army. As we entered the city, the people gave us a tumultuous welcome. On we went to the devastated enemy airfield, 'El Allo Ena' *(I thought this name a typo, but it is correct!)*, where we told to 'get our heads down' (to sleep) amid the burning enemy aircraft. Despite the detritus of war, we managed to get a few hours' sleep on the sand. When daylight came, we awoke to the cheery sound of the tea bucket. However, we did have a complaint. In between fitful snoozes we were conscious of the horrible smell of hastily buried corpses . . . over which we had been sleeping. Even under these conditions, we managed a (*typical military black-humoured*) laugh . . . The cry went up, 'Which of you bastards hasn't changed his socks??!!'

✠

An Interesting Souvenir

I found two of these propaganda pound notes in Tunis after my arrival there.

These are very interesting as they were dropped by German aircraft for use . . . or not . . . by the local civilian population. The Arabic on the reverse translates as:

> 'This is a specimen of English money which will be offered for food etc. Like the paper it is printed on, it is worthless. Refuse it and do everything you can to impede the Briton'

Another translator informed me that it actually states:

> 'If you inspect this banknote you will remember the time when it was worth ten times its present value in bright shiny gold. That was because at that time the strength of

> علامات الانحلال
>
> لو تأملت هذه الورقة المالية، لتذكرت ذلك الوقت الذي كان يدفع لك في مقابلها عشرة اضعاف وزنها من الذهب البرّاق والخلّاب.
>
> ذلك لأن هذه الوريقة كانت مضمونة من الامبراطورية العظمى بكل ما تمتلكه من قوى وغنى وأبهة.
>
> ولكن عظمتها زالت وغناها اندثر كالورق البالي.
>
> فما هي قيمة الورق اليوم؟ لابد انك ملمّ بذلك.
>
> ان كل يوم قد مرّ من ايام هذه الحرب التي أثارتها انكلترا، قد مزّق من قوى الامبراطورية الانكليزية. وكل معركة خسرتها انكلترا كانت سبباً في تدهور النقد البريطاني.
>
> ان اليوم قد قرب الذي سيرفض فيه الشحاذ المتسوّل على قارعة الطريق قبول الجنيه الانكليزي وان كنت ستعطيه اياه كهبة منك.
>
> ان الله قد اراد انحلال بريطانيا وسوف يكون...

the mighty British Empire supported such notes. But that greatness is fading as is the value of this worthless piece of paper. What is this note worth today? You certainly know the answer to that. With each passing day of this British inspired war, the strength of the Empire is depleted. Each battle that England loses causes a further weakening of its currency. The day draws near when even the beggars in the street will refuse the British banknote, even as a gift. Truly, Allah wills the collapse of Britain, which will surely come to pass.'

It is safe to say most of these were used to start the small night-time camp fires around which the Bedouin would sit.

> *These notes are now quite rare and can command three figures at auction!*
>
> *Those local civilians who helped the British forces were given 'chits in lieu' – paper forms ready signed which could be exchanged for money or goods.*

From here we set out on the last eight miles to Carthage, the famous ruined city of the Phoenicians, a place of villas, temples, and a Roman amphitheatre. It is a city steeped in history dating from long before the time of Christ and is a paradise for historians and archaeologists.

✚

Carthage

Carthage is situated in a depression right on the coastline of the Bay of Tunis and is dominated by three large white buildings. The Convent of the White Sisters, 'Maison Lavigerie', on the top of Byrsa Hill (occupied by about twelve nuns), the Monastery of the White Fathers, and close by, the impressive Cathedral.

I should imagine that everybody is familiar with the stories of Queen Dido, Hannibal and Scipio Africanus, so I hope that I may be forgiven for quoting a few historical facts regarding this ruined city.

> *Sadly, these days, not everyone has the benefit of a classical education, and Virgil's love story of Dido and*

Convent of the White Sisters on right, and Monastery of the White Fathers on left, both marked with 'X'.

CARTHAGE

Aeneas is largely forgotten. The Glory that was Carthage, Hannibal crossing the Alps with his elephants and his eventual defeat by Scipio, the razing of Carthage and the enslavement of its people are stories sadly known by few. In fact, the last stand of the Carthaginians in 146 BC was at the Temple of Eshmoon, on the very top of Byrsa Hill and under the Convent.

Carthage during the early centuries BC had become famous, and thus a threat to her neighbours. She possessed a formidable fleet of ships, plus a well-equipped army of many thousands with which the city state invaded Roman territory via Spain. You will of course have heard how Hannibal and his elephants crossed the Alps and advanced to within a few miles of the Eternal City – Rome itself. Naturally, Rome retaliated, invaded Carthage and destroyed it after the Third Punic War.

'Delenda est Carthago' – from the famous speech by Cato in the Senate of Rome ('Carthage must be destroyed').

These wars lasted from 264 to 146 BC. Like the much earlier Greek invasion of Troy, this was a war about trade, control of the Mediterranean and, especially during the first war, Sicily. The island was of course the springboard to launch the invasion of mainland Italy in 1943, again from North Africa. Interestingly, Scra will be found at the site of another famous Punic War battle later on . . .

La Maison Lavigerie, Convent of the White Sisters and the Cathedral of the White Fathers the Cathedral of Saint Louis, now the Acropolium of Carthage.

13

NURSING AT THE FRONTLINE

Convent marked with X.

CARTHAGE

St Louis Cathedral, the Cathedral of the White Fathers. Now known as the 'Acropolium', it is no longer used for worship, but instead hosts public events and concerts of Tunisian and classical music.

The Convent Hospital

I will now describe the convent of Maison Lavigerie that I mentioned earlier, which was used as a hospital by our unit. We established there a very efficient medical service.

The building contained several large rooms or 'salas', which converted into ideal hospital wards, having high ceilings, plenty of tall windows and white marble floors. There was plenty of fresh air from the sea and, above all, it was delightfully cool in the summer. When winter came, you can imagine our problem. There were no fireplaces, and what little heat there was emanated from two 'Aladdin' oil stoves at the end of the wards, and plenty of blankets! The beds themselves consisted of two ends joined by two side rods which were slipped through a piece of large hemmed canvas rather like a stretcher. These beds were an ingenious idea, and meant that we could quickly become mobile, move to a new site and become fully operational within an hour of arrival.

> *There were only two other Mobile Field Hospitals in the British Forces at the time that 31 MFH was founded: No.1 RAMC Mobile Field Hospital based in Cairo and 21 RAF Mobile Field Hospital, Scra's unit being only the second such RAF unit. They were based on the American system of 'MASH' (Mobile Army Surgical Hospital) units, although there had been a number of discussions post-Great War about the way in which medical assets should be utilized and positioned. The former Spanish Republican surgeon Douglas Jolley (Major RAMC in the Second World War) advocated a 'Three Point Forward System' with a No.1 Hospital at the furthest point possible forward near to the mobile front lines. The time lag of the*

THE CONVENT HOSPITAL

> *'flash to bang' (i.e. the injury to treatment time) which was proposed in the Great War was accepted amongst many as the single most important factor affecting mortality rates of the wounded. This is of course now known as the 'Golden Hour': the window for life-saving emergency treatment. I highly commend Douglas Jolley's book* Field Surgery in Total War, *details of which can be found in the bibliography.*

The Maison was situated on a hill overlooking the garden – such as it was – and commanded a panoramic view over the Bay of Tunis. It had been built over the site of the Temple of Venus, and it was said that in the basement could be seen an elaborate mosaic square of intricate design depicting Neptune and Sea Nymphs. Unfortunately, I never saw this.

> *It is interesting that although the Maisons of the White Fathers and White Sisters are now a museum and concert venue, I am yet to find any mention of such a mosaic! I have contacted them by email, and at time of writing am yet to receive any reply. Looking at the contemporary pictures of Byrsa Hill, it may be that the Maison has been demolished.*

Upon our arrival we found the whole of the ground floor occupied by a German medical team *(a Krieglazerett, or Field Hospital)*, with about one hundred and twenty patients and seventy medical staff. To avoid any stress and upheaval, our CO arranged for the top floor to be occupied by the British medical staff and patients. This remarkable feat was accomplished within the hour; wards were complete with beds, trolleys etc., and even a fully equipped operating theatre, all ready for the admission of new patients.

The hospital was actually in a deplorable state. The Germans had started working on the drains, but stopped before the town had surrendered. Many of the mattresses were covered in pus and had become breeding grounds for flies. The drains as they were just emptied out onto the ground outside either wall of the building.

On one side was a twelve-foot-square pit. There was no cover to it, and it contained all of the surgical, lavatorial and kitchen waste. You can imagine the state and indeed the smell! On the other side, the drains had failed, and the effluent seeped out of the ground over a wide area, making another ideal breeding ground for bugs and bacteria.

The ablutions in the main ward areas were blocked, and the hand-flush lavatories did not work. This of course meant more potential contamination and even more breeding grounds for flies and pathogens.

A gang of German prisoners were gainfully employed in digging out a new and full sewerage system, which then discharged out quite some distance from the hospital.

An admirable concession which was made by our CO upon arrival was that all German personnel and their patients should receive the same food rations as the British. This included such luxuries as cigarettes and NAAFI comforts.

I am sorry to say that this kind and humane gesture was abused. The German commandant was discovered destroying top secret documents which should have been given up at the time of surrender. There were no alternatives; the whole German unit and their patients were removed at once under an armed guard and sent to the prisoner of war camp. Such were the terms of war. The vacated quarters were then given back to the nuns – the White Sisters – who in their Christian manner had acted as nurses to the German wounded.

31 RAF MFH opened for business on 6th June with a bedstate (occupied beds) of eighty inpatients.

We liked and admired those kind, simple sisters, and they continued to receive and enjoy the subsidised food that we provided. Incidentally, I often came into contact with the Mother Superior, who spoke fairly good English. Eventually, it became a regular habit for me to visit her each Thursday afternoon for about an hour for a chat, which usually drifted into matters of biblical interest, she being fully aware that I was a Protestant.

I shall always remember one conversation. I was usually entertained in her own sitting room. This was a very austere apartment with whitewashed walls, an antiquated horsehair couch, a small table with a wooden chair, and a single iron bedstead. As is customary, a huge crucifix hung from one wall, and on another was a portrait of Christ with the traditional crown of thorns. During the conversation my eyes seem to centre on the portrait, and my hostess noticed this . . .

'So you like my picture?' she said out of politeness.

What could I say, as I have remarked that our conversations generally veered towards biblical subjects, which caused great interest and surprise to her?

'You know,' she said, 'you would make an excellent Catholic!'

'Thank you, Mother, for such a nice compliment!' I replied, then realised my opportunity and said, 'Every time I visit you I am fascinated by this picture. Here we are sitting side by side on this horsehair sofa, both of us admiring the same portrait; but what I see is not what you see, yet we are both looking at the same pathetic face.'

In a silent answer she smiled and clasped my hand.

Early mass was celebrated regularly each morning at 0415 hours, during our night duty, which came round about once a month for seven nights from 2000 hours to 0800 hours. One was kept well occupied with four-hourly temperatures and treatments, and sometimes there were less serious cases which required hourly or half hourly attention – by the way, it was assumed that no doctors were to be roused during the night. We were told that we were considered quite capable of treating any emergency – a comforting thought when you might be called on to look after two wards on your own, but I suppose that I was lucky.

At 0100, when all was quiet, it was the custom to have supper. This invariably consisted of hot dogs warmed on the Primus stove and lashings of hot sweet tea. The remainder of the night was usually quiet enough to enable me to write a letter to my wife or to resort to painting watercolours. The latter were scenes in miniature which I sent home, hoping that they would give some idea of my whereabouts. I may add here that the only means of lighting was one hurricane lamp. I leave it to you to imagine the difficulty of taking temperatures and pulse readings by the light of a single oil lamp. There was only one way: placing the lamp on the floor by each bed, kneeling down to read the thermometer and then entering the reading on the respective chart.

At 0415 it became my habit to listen for the shuffle of a nun's footstep along the marble corridor downstairs and to hear the gentle summons upon the cell doors, waking the nuns for prayer. This was the signal for me to put away my childish things, such as my paintings and letters, and to commence the routine of washbowls, temperatures, collection of specimens etc., and then to write my report for the day staff by 0800 hours. Finally, after all was done, we were away to bed.

Somebody once made a kind remark after hearing of my journeying: 'You've been on a ruddy "Cook's Tour", while we dodge the bombs!' It crossed my mind to mention to him three months without red meat, sleeping in tents on liquid mud and two feet of snow; running risks with inadequate instruments and drugs; and also dealing with infectious diseases, real killers, with very little protective clothing – but my lips remained sealed.

> *When the travel agent Thomas Cook was founded, their excursions were known as 'Cook's Tours'. When these extended to the Continent and indeed beyond, the name stuck. It then became the 'norm' for any convoluted trip to be known as a 'Cook's Tour'.*

By George!

Now, my helper on ward duty was a typical London Cockney, born and bred in 'Walwerf' (Walworth), well within earshot of Bow Bells, and he was quite a distinctive character, hefty, rough and kind-hearted, and the driver of one of our Bedford lorries.

I remember one particular night returning to our quarters, tired after a busy day on the surgical wards. It was getting dark, and those who were off duty had gone into Tunis. The quarters were empty, and I wasn't feeling all that cheerful. After making my bed I sat down to write a letter home. After a while the door was suddenly kicked open and in strode George the Cockney.

'Wotcher cock! Are you going to bed?'

'No, not yet', I replied.

'I may as well join yer then!' he said cheerfully.

I nodded in acquiescence.

We sat on the edge of our beds, and the conversation became interesting; in fact, I was glad of his company. I cannot remember what prompted us to discuss any particular subject; perhaps it was something to do with 'Civvy Street' and the time before we joined up.

'Yus', he said thoughtfully, 'that reminds of the time when I did a stretch.'

'A stretch?' I questioned

'Blimey!' he said surprised, 'don't say you've never 'eard the word before? On the Moor, in the Clink, in PRISON!'

He shouted the last word with vehemence.

I was taken by surprise and somewhat shocked by such a definite admission.

'Whatever for?' I enquired.

'Well, if you must know, pin yer lugholes (ears) back and I'll tell yer!'

He continued, 'It was like this. I was walking one afternoon down The Cut (*a street in Walworth market*), when I saw a smashing car, unattended. The driver's window was down, and the ignition key was on the dashboard, and there was nobody near, so . . . in I jumps. But as I put my dainty mitts on the starter, I felt a hand on my shoulder . . . I turned to look into the face of a copper! He nabbed me, and pulled me out by the scruff of my neck, and that's how I got a stretch!'

When I heard this, I really thought it was one of his 'yarns', but in utter surprise, I could only say 'George!!!', with my chin almost on the floor.

The reason for relating this story – which is perfectly true – is to show that humour and sympathy to patients is sometimes expressed by the most unlikely person – which to the medical staff was always a great asset.

Whenever a serious case was admitted to the ward on a trolley, extreme care was taken to transfer the patient to a prepared bed. He had to be lifted gently, and George was always there to assist.

'What the hell have they done to you, cock?' he would say. 'Never mind, stick this fag in yer mowf, and I'll bring yer a cup of char. Don't worry, I'll look after yer, mate!'

Even during 'Last Offices', the laying out and preparing of a body, George would be there.

Relating this story reminds me of another similar incident: a case of reaction after an unpleasant moment.

A young lad aged about twenty had been bought in, found drowned. The body was very dirty and caked in mud. In George I had a very capable assistant, who carried the body in his arms just as one would carry a baby.

'Now come on old chum hold your chin up while I wash yer face', he said. 'Yer can't go to God with a dirty neck can ya? What would your mother say?'

George was married and had two young children. He slept in the bed next to mine, and I would leave money and personal items lying around without hesitation. Also, I never witnessed a quarrel amongst my pals at any time that the Mobile Field Hospital existed.

This was indeed true comradeship.

The sequel to this narrative occurred a couple of years after the war. My wife and I spent an enjoyable holiday by coach to the Wye Valley and the famous Hereford Cathedral. Our thoughtful coach driver, wherever possible, avoided the busy main roads, so as to enable the passengers to see the pastoral views. One particular road we followed was hilly and narrow, only just wide enough for two cars to pass each other, but impossible for two coaches to pass. We slowly made our way to the summit, from where we could see another coach approaching from the opposite direction.

We had seen some lay-bys at intervals along the road, but at the crest we could only discern one such gap between us and the next climb. The driver slowed down with caution, but the other coach was approaching us . . . at speed! The objective was the next lay-by, halfway between us, and both drivers were determined to get there first.

With a screeching of brakes, the two coaches came to a sudden halt, with not a hundred feet between them. Angry shouting ensued, and both drivers clambered down from their seats, the confrontation very nearly ending in fisticuffs! We were seated near the back, and everyone stood up to witness the scene.

Finally our coach pulled into the lay-by, not without some difficulty, the passengers horrified by the amount of obscene language.

It was at this point I was able to observe the driver of the other coach, and I suddenly turned to my wife: 'Well, I'll be . . . it's George!!'

I had recognized his voice and his 'phraseology'. Sadly, I failed to get near to the window fast enough to hail him. That was the other side of my old friend.

'What a horrible man', commented our fellow passengers.

There was only one person on this coach who would have been delighted to have wrung his hand instead of his neck. We never met again, but I will always remember him.

> *I believe I have traced 'George' as George Harrup, who is listed on the 1939 Register as a 'lorry driver'. I was led to this name via a letter to Scra from one of the Medical Officers, Peter Dinnick, of whom I have presented a pen picture in another chapter.*

✥

Digging for Pleasure

During periods of leisure, I used to examine the surrounding ruins and rubble, and whatever was found could nearly always be identified by a certain monk at the monastery who was an expert archaeologist of some renown.

I think the most interesting find was a portion (or 'sherd') of a bowl. You will observe from my drawings the imprint of a lion and on the reverse side the thumbprint of the potter. There is some doubt as to its origin – my friend at the monastery suggested that it could have been made circa 650 BC, as King Gyges had gold coins stamped with a lion. Another suggestion was that it might be of Spanish origin (Philip of Spain invaded Tunis in about 1535). On the other hand, the British Museum dates it to the 6th century

With regard to the two pieces of early Roman oil lamps, you will note the burnt section where the wick emerges. It was the custom to burn olive oil, but on closer examination one sees no stain on the interior.

Whilst I was in Carthage an old man made a complete full-size model lamp for me. It was beautifully designed, depicting Christ's head and shoulders. It was made of clay and in two sections, then baked in the sun. The occasion once arose for us to make use of it, when there was a power failure. A lamp wick was placed in the aperture, and olive oil was used as fuel. The result was highly successful, the only disadvantage being that, when the flame was extinguished, the wisp of smoke gave off a most obnoxious smell.

Another fragment I found was of very early origin. It was made of very thin clay on which was inscribed a tree and a bird – the bird represents the God Tanit or Tanith or Tanit Pene Baal (the Face of Baal). She was the chief Goddess of Carthage. Punic depictions show her wrapped in a double pair of wings, much like her Egyptian counterparts Isis and Hathor. This has been identified as part of a pot.

Scra in the ruins of ancient Carthage.

Another interesting specimen is a Roman or Phoenician bread weight used to weigh the flour sufficient to make pasta or a pancake. It can be described as a circular piece of cornelian marble about one inch in diameter and half an inch thick, weighing two ounces.

Carthage was originally a great Tyrian or Phoenician colony. It was successively invaded and destroyed by the Romans, the Goths and the Vandals. Thus you may appreciate the difficulty of identifying relics, coins or the sherds of pottery which abound and which can be found simply by disturbing the sand with one's foot. I found many interesting pieces, including those illustrated.

Sadly, not all these finds made it into the bags I received from the now anonymous neighbour. We are left with Scra's excellent drawings of what must have been very interesting pieces

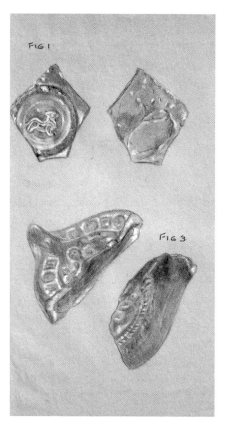
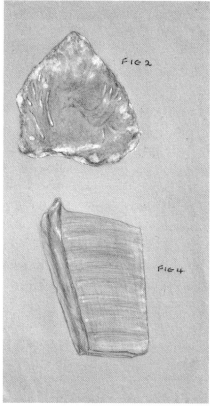

Fig 1

This shows the base of a small bowl with an indentation of a lion. The British Museum believes that this fragment is late Roman 'A' period ware, dating from the late 5th or early 6th century AD.

This was produced in considerable quantities in North Africa almost to the time of the Arab conquest – 670 to 698 AD. You will observe on the reverse side the imprint of the potter's thumb and nail.

Fig 2

A much earlier specimen of decoration on a sherd, depicting a tree and bird. Early 3rd century AD. It has been suggested that the bird represents the Goddess of Carthage, Tanit.

Fig 3

Two portions of early Roman oil lamps. Note the scorch marks made by the flame of the burning wick one of the pieces. The protrusion on the other piece served as a type of handle or thumb rest.

Fig 4

This shows a rare portion of a heavy water or wine jar, laminated with possibly three layers of clay. It is suggested that the probable reason for this is to give it strength, or possibly some form of insulation.

In addition to these interesting specimens, I discovered several small Roman coins, far too small to illustrate. Some were a mere fraction under half an inch. They are well worn, encrusted and difficult to identify. The finest of these features the laurel-wreathed profile of 'Probus', probably from around the year 237 AD.

There was very little entertainment to be had when we were off duty. There was of course, the sandy beach, and one could swim in the warm sea. The other alternative was to stroll two or three miles to the famous French colony of artists, Sidi-Bou-Said. This was a delightfully picturesque Moorish village of ultra-modern (*for 1943!*) villas, with the typical atmosphere of an artist's paradise, beautifully laid out gardens with lawns, fountains, and masses of exotic flowers.

We noticed one gleaming white house of stone, one of those places one often reads about but seldom sees. Passing behind the villa we observed with some surprise an impressive ornamental wrought iron gate, which revealed a haven of colour and a silent pool, where stood three flamingos, their long delicate legs of pinky red reflected in the clear water. It was breathtaking in comparison with the arid waste of dust and the ruins of Carthage which were just a couple of hours walk away.

On other evenings a few of us would saunter down to a certain villa-cum-bar in the small village of Byrsa-Bougie. Incidentally, the bar was named Le Pescadou (the fisherman), although our interpretation was slightly different! It was hidden amongst the old eucalyptus and mimosa trees, and to complete the picture there was a wall completely covered by a mass of purple bougainvillea.

It was not only the delightful perfumes and the botanical colours which prompted us to visit this place; we simply wanted to sample the local vintage. The surroundings were certainly peaceful and attractive, the only sounds coming from the creaking pulley above the ancient well, the plop of water when the bucket was dropped, and sometimes the donkey braying in protest. It was a perfect atmosphere in which to sample the nectar of the gods. A pretty young French girl came forward when she saw we were comfortably seated on the hard wooden stools and presented us with a card showing the various wines obtainable and their respective prices. Naturally, we sampled the cheapest as a starter, Algerian red. We knew that it was always the custom of the Arabs to add a dash of water, but we dared not risk it! Luckily, we obtained a sealed bottle of soda water, but even with this addition we did not relish the acid vinegar taste. There were other wines to be tried – Raki and a Vermouth of a rather poor vintage – and of course absinthe. However, we enjoyed the stroll and the pleasant surroundings which gave us a break from the usual everyday routine. It was a pity that we did not enjoy the wine, but we walked back slowly through the shadows of the trees made by the burnished gold of the sinking sun, listening to the chorus of the crickets. And so to bed.

Occasionally we were given the privilege of half a day of freedom, that is provided we could be spared. This gave us the opportunity of spending the afternoon in Tunis, some eight miles away. The local train service between Carthage and the city was good and the fare reasonable. The coaches were similar to the trams one used to find in most of the French towns, and during the rush hour passengers clung onto the outside with their fingertips. We often wondered whether they ever paid their fares.

Tunisian French franc note.

The train entered at the main boulevard and continued right through the town as far as the Casbah, the native section of the city which the troops were forbidden to enter.

So these few hours away from the hospital enabled us to relax and come into contact with French civilians. We had the opportunity to window-gaze in the many shops and stores, which were typically French in their displays. Unfortunately, the prices were far beyond the reach of our pockets. The Boulevard was very wide, and down the centre was a stretch of pavement lined with various trees, in between which stood stalls with floral displays. We really felt that we were back in civilisation once more.

One afternoon, three of us ventured into one of the side streets, drawn by the large caption on the side of a building – 'Cinema'. This was a great temptation. The film was Errol Flynn in 'The Pirates', so in we went. It was a dingy theatre, and smelly too. When we entered, the film was in progress, so we carefully felt our way down the gangway, managing to find space on a wooden bench without a backrest. We must have entered about halfway through the main film. At the finish the lights went up, and we had a shock. The whole place was filled with natives! A nod was a sufficient signal for us to beat a hurried exit. We returned to Carthage for a check of our possessions and a bath, plus a complete change of clothing and a damn good laugh. It was very foolish of us, and we should have realised the risk we took of being knifed and mutilated, simply for the possession of our paybooks and uniforms valued at £10 (*some £600 today*), which would have then been passed to the enemy.

The Roman hall of justice

Exploring the ruins near the theatre of Carthage one day, I found hidden in the undergrowth a circular mound about 30 feet in diameter. Treading warily, fearing to be caught up on the sharp needles of the cacti, I found this to be a domed roof open at the top with a large circular aperture. This particular structure was commonly found in the larger Roman villas, the purpose of which was to allow in light, air and coolness from the temperature above ground level, as found later on in the ancient city of Pompeii. In some villas the roof was either square or oblong, and immediately below was invariably an ornamental shallow pond, sometimes decorated with either a statue or some other form, which served to provide drinking water.

Wending my way through the vegetation, I was delighted to discover the entrance to a stone staircase. Treading carefully amid the crumbling debris, I descended the twenty or so steps with caution. The walls were of sandstone of a yellowish tinge, which showed signs of dampness causing patches of mildew, somehow resembling the grain usually seen in wood. Finally reaching the bottom step, I had to turn left to another shorter staircase, which led me into brilliant daylight in a spacious circular chamber. There was evidence that someone had been here before, as much of the rubble had been removed, revealing a stone paved floor. Near the centre there appeared to be a slightly raised platform, and upon closer examination I observed three small holes in the floor, presumably for the feet of a tripod.

Several pillars ranged the circular wall, some of white marble, some cornelian, and others green serpentine. I also found pieces of Egyptian pottery. Above these columns I could discern oblong tablets which showed traces of names, possibly of Gods or senators. I also noticed that some had been removed.

It was cold and deathly quiet down here. Several lizards started away into the crevices amongst the fallen stones. I did not stay long

but returned to the surface up a similar staircase on the opposite side to the one by which I had entered. I then reached the entrance to confront the glare and intense heat of daylight. I proceeded towards the hospital and on the way I met the gardener from a nearby cemetery. He took great pains to explain in detail the history and purpose of this fascinating chamber. It was the Roman Hall of Justice, he told me. Prisoners would descend by one flight of steps, pass before the magistrate for judgement and depart up the stairs on the other side.

The tripod which fitted into the platform mentioned earlier once held an ornate brass or copper bowl of water, perhaps giving hope to the malefactor by the significant act of washing of the hands, as Pontius Pilate had once done; hence the remark so often heard today – 'I wash my hands of the entire (or whole) affair' – which comes down to us all these centuries later. Interestingly, the Amphitheatre itself was not too far away, for those who were found guilty.

This is now identified as 'The Rotunda of Damous El Karita'. It was an early Basilica, and one of the most important Christian monuments in the Mediterranean. Sadly, it is also one the most abused and poorly

Twilight in the convent chapel.

known. The 'Roman Hall of Justice' of which Scra speaks was an Ambulatory of one of the two Byzantine churches here, contained the remains of Christian saints and was a site of pilgrimage in ancient times. Modern pictures of the site match Scra's painting exactly.

The evening was still warm, with a slight breeze drifting from the placid sea which was enough to disturb the nearby palm fronds, which seemed to blend with the solitude of a deserted Roman street in the ruined city. It was to this place that I often retired, where peacefulness and tranquillity prevailed after the energy and bustle of routine duty in the hospital.

Looking across the bay from where I usually sat, the silhouette of Bor Kornime – the mountain of the two heads – showed sharply defined against the ever-changing hues of the twilight sky; this spot was full of the atmosphere of Roman life centuries ago. The doorposts of white marble, showing the apertures where the metal hinges of the huge wooden doors once hung, still stood like sentinels.

The deep gutters on either side of the wide thoroughfare had miniature stone bridges built over them at the entrance of each villa to allow a dry entry. The remains of the inner walls were festooned with painted figures and colourful designs, and although these were faded, and the

The Mountain of the Two Heads from the Convent.

intricate designs of the mosaic floors somewhat damaged by the passing of the centuries, it was all still beautiful to look upon.

I would then stroll leisurely down under the archway into the interior of the ancient theatre, on the stage of which a few broken columns were still standing.

I often stood alone in silence in the centre and let my imagination wander, standing like an actor or patrician about to deliver his speech even at a whisper, which would be echoed back to the Roman orator from the tiers of marble seats towering up high above; some were still intact, and yet smooth and cool. Then in my imagination my thoughts would fly to the days of feasts, speeches and plays, with the roars of applause from the plebeians.

Well, I became a spectator there too! I was one of the 2,000 troops assembled to listen to the oratory of the leader of our country during the war, Winston Churchill himself. I stood upon the highest spot on the rim of the vast auditorium listening to his stirring speech. The acoustics were perfect; his sniff, and the intake of his breath came loud and clear without a single loudspeaker or microphone. [In the picture above, X marks the spot where Churchill stood to make his speech.] The theatre came to life again; then you realised that those Romans and Carthaginians were very clever people.

I wonder if a name is still to be seen to this day, carved in capital letters on one of the pillars which stood on the stage, chiselled by our carpenter.

31 MFH Chums in the Amphitheatre.

No, it was not his surname but that of his hometown, Canterbury, where his thoughts always strayed. This may be the only evidence of the sojourn of the British troops left in this most historic place, and it in no way desecrated such a venerable site.

On another similar evening I sat upon the fallen ornamented capital from a broken column, intent on writing my weekly letter home and taking in the panoramic view and the stillness of solitude. Suddenly I thought I saw a movement, something white in the villa nearby. I looked again, but there was nothing, so I returned to my letter, thinking it was an optical illusion or just my imagination. Some time elapsed, then quite suddenly someone spoke to me from behind . . .

'Good evening.'

There to my surprise stood a tall Arab, dressed in his white flowing mantle. I suppose I must have looked startled, as I had never before seen a soul near here at this time of day.

He was tall, handsome and about thirty years old. Every inch a cultured gentleman. He asked if he might rest awhile beside me. Naturally, I became interested and granted permission.

During our conversation he mentioned he had just returned from college recess. He spoke of England as one who had lived there, which made me think he had had an English education and had returned home for a while. I really enjoyed our chat on many subjects of mutual interest. We met several times at the same place in about the same time, and finally he arranged a meeting in Tunis to show me the famous mosque, a privilege seldom extended to the 'unbeliever'.

When I came out I asked myself whether, if only Christians expressed themselves in their beliefs as ardently as the Muslims, the world would surely be a happier place. He bade me goodbye and we placed hands on heart, touched our lips and then our brows in true Arab salutation and departed never to meet again. I believe he told me the meaning of the salutation was, 'From my heart, my lips, my mind – Allah go with you.'

I am not certain of the exact words, but no matter, the action without words is of prime importance.

Medical Duty

Returning to the thoughts of ward duties, I recall incidents both sad and amusing. I found medical cases particularly interesting; there was such a wide variety of ailments to be treated.

It was instilled into us during training at the General Hospital that if you gained the confidence of your patients, they will respond to your treatments. Another adage was to trace the cause and endeavour to remove it. These are words of wisdom, which more often than not brought amazing results. You became attached to those in your care, got to know their anxieties and fears, learned about their families and the kind of life they led before they became involved in the 'nation's liabilities'.

One felt a sense of achievement in assisting them back to a healthy, normal life – or on the other hand, a sadness and disappointment as one saw other patients who simply slipped through one's fingers.

I remember one such incident which still mystifies me. This happened to a particularly nice chap, who liked to show me the latest photographs from home.

'That's my kid Jimmy and he's grand boy. Nearly as tall as his mum now!'

This was a typical case where we noticed he was slipping away. In this instance he could put out his hand for someone to hold. Poor chap . . . miles away from kith and kin. That's the sort of disappointment to the doctor and to those who looked after him which one felt; in spite of the intensive care we gave we felt that we had somehow failed.

I gathered up his belongings – the letters, the photos and other mementoes that I knew he treasured – to be handed over to our CO. Underneath the empty box that served as a bedside locker, I stooped to pick up a small trinket. Whilst I was getting up from kneeling position,

I noticed a vapour pass from the body. I would not say I was afraid, but it was something beyond my ken. That evening, a small group of us – including two doctors – were having a quick break; that meant a mug of tea and a quiet smoke. I remarked about the vapour I had seen. I suggested to the two doctors that this might be evaporation caused by the cooling-down process of the body.

'That was the spirit leaving the body', came the answer.

All the other jaws dropped in amazement at such a definite statement, especially knowing that both doctors held no belief in the hereafter or had any religious feelings whatsoever. Well, it sounds imaginative, and yet I can honestly say that I saw this manifestation – if you like to call it such – on two other occasions. It was they who were dead serious about it all, so I shall leave it to you – perhaps you may have an answer?

A further example of gaining the patient's trust brings to mind the case of a serious condition after an operation.

Again, this happened whilst on night duty. Morphia had been given by the sister before 2200 hrs, and the state of sedation should have been sufficient for him to sleep the night through. About 0330 hrs the silence on the ward was broken by the crying of this man. He had awakened, was in pain and pleaded to be given another injection. I was unable to comply. No instruction for a further dose was prescribed on his chart, and I regretfully told him so. I felt sorry for him, especially seeing him in such a distressed condition. He pleaded for anything to relieve the pain, so I told him I would give him something and risk the chance of getting into serious trouble, but he must on no account tell anyone. I gave him a small dose of medicine usually prescribed for an upset stomach containing a small amount of chlorodyne diluted with water.

'Now drink it slowly, and you will go to sleep, and by so doing you will taste more fully the flavour.'

Whether it was a case of autosuggestion I can't say, but he slept the remainder of the night – deeply gratifying to both of us. Full details were recorded in my night report. The operation concerned was for the extraction of shrapnel from his leg.

It is interesting that Scra uses the term 'shrapnel'. This in its original form was an explosive shell containing 360 steel ball bearings which burst above the enemy troops. It was invented by a Lieutenant John Shrapnel during the Napoleonic War, hence 'Shrapnel's shells'. It later came to be applied to any pieces of shell casing or lumps of metal from shells, grenades, bombs or even pieces of crashed aeroplanes!

I must mention here that the hospital would not have functioned so efficiently were it not for our two nursing sisters. I shall refer to them only as 'Sister A' and 'Sister B'. Their responsibility was the efficient control of medical and surgical wards and the nursing staff, including the operating theatre. Although they were disciplinarians they also had superb knowledge of the medical and surgical world; yet one could always detect sympathy and kindness beneath their superior rank. They were admired and respected by all members of the staff.

It takes great courage for two women to live and work amongst men, sharing the same conditions and privations, devoid of all the necessities of femininity. I spent many months with 'Sister B' in surgical, and her guidance gave me valuable experience, which served me very well on many future occasions. The following is just one of many incidents I remember so well.

One day, she said, 'I wish I had some hair rollers!'

Here we were, right out in the blue yonder, on the edge of the North African desert. However, I had an idea and went to our electrician and scrounged a length of rubber-covered thin wire. This I cut into 6-inch lengths to make some form of hair curlers. I'd like to think this small gesture made her happy. I don't think it made all that difference to her appearance, since she possessed a well-shaped head of naturally wavy hair, which always looked immaculate. I suppose it's natural for one to desire something more, even if one already knows it's simply an impossibility. Under the scorching sun any one of us often wished for a glass of cold water and nothing more.

Now, on the other hand if you displeased the Sisters, beware! Their tongues were mightier than any sword – however, they were not often employed.

I recall one particular instance involving an aggressive Sergeant being admitted. He was an illiterate bully who could not forget his three chevrons of authority. He only suffered from a minor complaint, yet he failed to appreciate the luxury of lying in a comfortable bed with clean sheets and being waited on. All he had been accustomed to was parade-ground language. I happened to be on duty at night at the time, and it was customary for the sister of the ward to pop in to check with the person on duty any special treatments necessary during the night. The clinical charts of every patient were scrutinised, and the sister halted when she came to the Sergeant's name.

'He's been in here three days.'

'Yes, Sister', I replied

'I think he can be discharged in the morning. There doesn't seem to be too much wrong with him. Give him one ounce of castor oil at 1000 hrs . . . and at what time do you have supper?'

'One o'clock, Sister.'

'Give the Sergeant a mug of hot tea – if he's asleep, wake him.'

'But Sister . . . ?' I queried,

'No buts, that's an order! That should cleanse him and teach him in the future never to swear at an officer!'

These instructions were carried out, and the patient learned his lesson – much to his discomfort. This was the only time I witnessed such harsh treatment. Knowing Sister B, I think she was sorry afterwards.

> *The effect of 2 ounces of castor oil, and then a mug of tea later would ensure that the sergeant's bowels would have been completely purged of any and all matter therein. He would have had to spend rather a long time on the lavatory!*

Now Sister A was very different in both looks and manner; she was short in stature, not quite so feminine, and with a clipped and commanding way of speaking. Both sisters were capable in an emergency and possessed expert knowledge equal to any doctor. Sister A, although severe, was approachable, kind and sympathetic.

When the youngest male nurse, a boy of nineteen, sacrificed his life in devotion to duty to his patients during the hepatitis epidemic, she was grief-stricken. During an overseas leave of fourteen days she made it a priority to visit his parents in Edinburgh and offer her condolences. Sister A reached the zenith of her career by becoming the supreme

MEDICAL DUTY

commander of the Royal Air Force Nursing Service. When she retired she was deservedly rewarded by being made a Dame of the British Empire. She will always be remembered.

So here we had two of the finest leaders of a kind that you would rarely meet in any London hospital today. No words of gratitude will be sufficient to express our admiration and affection for them both. The last time I met Sister A was in Rome in 1945, and together we visited all the historical sites whilst on a three-month course of art and archaeology. She made a wonderful companion. After a critical illness she was sadly 'called to a higher authority' shortly after her retirement.

> *After a little research I have found that 'Sister A' was in fact Dame Veronica Ashworth DCBE, RRC. She had trained at St Bartholomew's Hospital in London from 1930. She qualified as a State Registered Nurse in 1934, after which she moved to Leeds, becoming a State Certified Midwife in 1935. The next year, she joined Princess Mary's Royal Air Force Nursing Service, and after RAF training was appointed to permanent status in 1937. As well as serving in Tunis and Italy with the 21st Mobile Field Hospital RAF, she also served as Matron at RAF Wroughton and RAF Uxbridge. In August 1963 she was appointed Matron in Chief of the PMRAFNS and was promoted to Air Commandant. Interestingly, when a Group Captain, she qualified as a parachutist, one of only a select few in PMRAFNS.*
>
> *Dame Veronica had been appointed Royal Red Cross 1st Class in 1959, Queen's Honorary Nursing Sister 1963 and in the 1964 New Year's honours list Dame Commander of the Order of the British Empire. She died on 12 January 1977.*
>
> *'Sister B', it appears, was a PMRAFNS Nurse by the name of Helen Jones, though there appears to be little information about her available, other than that she was commissioned as a Sister from the Reserve on 7 July 1942.*
>
> *Although a Royal Air Force Temporary Nursing Service was founded in 1918 alongside the inception of the Royal*

NURSING AT THE FRONTLINE

Air Force, it did not become permanent until 1921, and PMRAFNS received its Royal prefix in 1923.

Like the QAIMNS, PMRAFNS were only of equivalent RAF rank status and used the nursing titles Staff Nurse, Sister, Senior Sister and Matron until 1943, when the PMRAFNS were allowed rank insignia corresponding to the RAF rank structure.

As a mobile field hospital, the time came when we were ordered to move. The day of our departure from our friends at the convent drew near. I had previously arranged to make my final visit to the Mother Superior on a Thursday afternoon as usual. The day came all too soon, and I had a feeling of sadness that I should never see them again. I had become really attached to them.

One of the nuns, a kind and friendly Frenchwoman named Sister Theresa, spoke fairly good English. She was interested in all forms of art, including fine lace needlework, and yet in spite of all her skill I often saw her at work in the convent garden. Her long white robe would be pulled up between her legs and fastened to her waist with a large safety pin. She would be engrossed in her share of the manual work in the vegetable patch, usually with a smile of peace and contentment on her face.

On this day I was received by the Reverend Mother and escorted into a large reception room before the assembly of all the nuns. The Mother Superior then addressed the assembly as follows:

'Our dear friend is leaving us and we shall miss him. We bid him Godspeed and farewell. We shall always remember him and should like him to be comforted by the knowledge that we shall pray each morning at our early mass at 0415 for his safe return to his loved ones. There is only one condition that we ask: we should like him to promise, if God answers our prayers that directly he reaches home, he will write and tell us that our prayers have been answered.'

I solemnly promised that I would do so. Nearly two years later, when I had reached home after wandering many miles through a number of different countries, I sent a letter to those kind souls assuring them that their prayers had been truly answered. Months went by and no reply came. After a year I traced a Nursing Sister from our time in Carthage,

MEDICAL DUTY

The Nuns of the White Sisters teaching carpet-making to young children of all denominations at the convent in Carthage.

and during our conversation she mentioned that she had returned to Carthage and the convent, but alas, the whole community had died of typhoid. This calamity had occurred a few months after our departure. This was a sad ending, and yet for them it was a fulfilment which they richly deserved as an offering to God.

We were now told we were moving to a secluded spot by the sea to relax and recuperate. The hospital had been posted to Hammamet.

Hammamet

This was a small Arab village. In those days it boasted just one small hotel by the seashore, the Hotel de Golf, so different from the many erected today to cater for the vast number of tourists who come to this modern health resort. We received orders to move here in late July.

On our way to the new site we passed slowly through the village, fascinated by the many traders making their wares in full view of passers-by: carpet weavers, a potter and his wheel, a carpenter, a fruit vendor and not forgetting the wool dyer. We noticed that between the stone houses were lines of rustic poles upon which hung large hanks of dyed wool in wonderful shades drying in the sun.

These were used in the manufacture of their famous carpets. It was early evening when we eventually completed the task of erecting ridge tents in which to sleep. There was still sufficient daylight for us to explore our new surroundings, so a few of us turned our attention to the deserted hotel. It was obvious Jerry had left rather hurriedly. Papers and personal belongings were strewn about the floor. Nothing of importance was found; a few photographs of nude females on the walls, plus the usual trash always to be found when a unit moves out. However, I found an attractive brass vase lying on top of an orange box which had one time served as a bedtime locker, alongside the remains of a camp bed. The richest find was when we walked out into the fading light into the neglected garden. I discovered a fair-size tree heavily laden with fruit similar to apricots but stoneless, the colour of a ripe orange that appeared fluorescent against the darkening shadows.

Waking early to look through the flaps of the tent, we saw the dancing sea in the morning sunlight and heard the whisper of the receding tide, along with the distant voices and lost laughter from the bathers. Here was peace and freedom.

HAMMAMET

The wool dyers of Hammamet.

The temptation was too much and, naked as the day we were born, my companion and I ran down the shimmering sands into the warm, refreshing sea. It was simply idyllic. As we had erected only two small tented wards, there were few patients. Most days were spent in the water or reclining in the shade of the date palms, where we found chameleons and lizards, which were hard to distinguish among the stones. In addition, we kept a sharp eye for a lethal object resembling a highly polished spinning top – to pick one up could be fatal. We were told by the Arabs that many of their children had been severely injured, and some killed, by these terrible weapons. They were small anti-personnel bombs that had been scattered around half-hidden by the enemy, so that they could only be spotted when the sun reflected a glint from the highly polished metal.

After a while an order was issued that all personnel must be able to dive and swim, as there was every possibility that we would be involved in the upcoming invasion. A floating platform of empty oil drums and a couple of planks of wood were constructed and towed to a deep pool. So clear was the water that one could see the fish swimming around the bottom. In fact, it was such a beautiful spot that we always referred to it as the blue lagoon.

Regrettably, this ideal rest camp was soon to end. They were happy days until misfortune struck, when two of our personnel were lost, to deep regret, both tragically killed in separate road accidents over two days. What had previously been leisure became monotony.

One of the dead was a Squadron Leader, a brilliant surgeon held in the highest esteem by all staff. I like to remember him as he was on the first day we came into close contact. We had set up camp near the small village of Maison Carré, a few miles from Algiers, having landed on the Good Friday and arrived there on Easter Saturday. That evening, he invited anyone wishing to celebrate Easter communion to a service in a brickfield close by at 1100 hours on Sunday morning. A few of the lads thoughtfully constructed an altar of rough bricks, but had no intention attending the service themselves.

In the event, about ten of us were present, and the service was short and simple – no sacramental wine, no hymns, just the dedication and the administration. He took a piece of bread and broke a piece off before each of us. The service was conducted with sincerity and humility, and he became one of us. This is how I will always remember him.

A corporal clerk from our dental clinic became the second victim. He was a young and conscientious assistant, popular with the lads. These tragedies affected us all. Gone now was the attraction of this beautiful place. Little did we know that our next move would be to the other extreme, the solitude of the desert. I think the most enjoyable surprise that followed, and it is worth mentioning, is something that happened on a certain Friday. There was little variation in our diet, and we could hardly believe it when someone called out that morning:

'Fish and chips today, lads!'

This sounded like an imaginary dinner. However, it turned out that we really were talking about the great and rare delicacy. Everyone was ordered off the beach, but told to be ready to dive in at given signal. Six chaps tossed detonators into the sea, and as a result of these small explosions, fish were stunned and floated to the surface; in went the swimmers to gather a rich harvest. It was a sumptuous meal, but we had to be careful to remove all the skin, which was now it was tinged a bright golden colour, since it was very poisonous.

Our stay at Hammamet was short, only about two months, and in the end we were not sorry to leave. The next move was to a desert site just outside that holy city of the Muslims, Kairouan.

✠

Kairouan

This is the scenic view from our site painted in watercolour while on night duty. The only light being one hurricane lamp. The other three views are from the town.

Waving a fond farewell on 15th September, we had left Hammamet to commence another journey, this time to Kairouan, far inland towards the desert. It is the second Islamic holy city and is situated 100 miles south of Tunis, and like most other places in North Africa it has an historic past. Why we were sent to this desolate place about two miles from the actual city amid the sand and scrub, only the Lord knows!

Above, opposite and overleaf pages: *Kairouan, an old watchtower and the Casbah.*

KAIROUAN

KAIROUAN

We had to endure tropical heat of 100 degrees in the shade in a fully equipped tented hospital with very few patients, and for some time without bread or fresh meat, the semi-hard army biscuits and tinned meat being our mainstays. It was to be expected that the spirits of all began to flag.

There was very little recreation; even a chance to visit the city was frowned upon by the commanding officers of both Army and RAF units. Their main concern was of course for the safety of the personnel. Espionage was rife; here as in Tunis, an Arab was paid £5 for a service pay book and a further £5 for a uniform, but nothing extra for a body.

I remember that soon after we arrived the RAF police paid us a visit and informed us that a lorry with food rations had been hijacked, part of the load consisting of half a tonne of sugar. In their efforts to trace the missing stores they raided the city and to their amazement, and quite by accident, discovered a second city, an underground one, which the police described as being like a complicated rabbit warren. The narrow and indescribably filthy alleyways of the old city below were ventilated by air shafts, which also provided a glimpse of daylight. Its main advantage was the coolness compared with the heat above. The RAF Regiment moved in and the whole place was searched, but nothing was ever found.

This brings to mind a similar incident which happened later in Naples. Again, a lorry was stolen, this time containing 500 pale grey blankets, and within a couple of days the police noticed that the Italian girls were wearing smart coats and skirts, made of course from the missing material! Orders were given to the military police to retrieve any such garments from their wearers. This they did, causing much merriment among the spectators and loud screams from the guilty parties.

To resume . . . now it happened at the time of the missing load of rations that I had two police officers as patients. During a conversation with them I mentioned that I would like to visit the ancient and mysterious city below ground. They warned me against such a foolhardy venture, saying I'd never come out alive! However, they said that when they were back on duty they would escort me through the Souk (*Casbah, market*), a promise which they fulfilled.

I felt important, although dwarfed by the stalwart six-footers who were fully armed, as we walked through the narrow bazaars of the merchants and traders. It was a casual tour, as we strolled slowly but never halted. Gone was the romantic mysticism that I once imagined.

It became necessary for guards to be posted at the hospital day and night, however, and we could see the city from the camp, a dim outline of white buildings dominated by the tall watchtower and the minaret. Between us lay two miles of desert which was occasionally disturbed by the zigzag moment of the jerboas (*commonly known as 'desert rats'*). These are mouse-like creatures with long tufted tails and very long hind legs. On one occasion we organised a shoot, the first man to hit one of the creatures winning the jackpot, usually valued at five pounds. There was only one condition: we were allowed just three shots with a rifle. Of course, nobody ever won the prize, and the money was eventually paid into the comforts fund.

A custom, and perhaps a necessity, was when on night duty to step outside the stuffy ward, just a few yards for a breath of fresh air and a look up into the dark blue vault of the sky to observe the galaxy of stars brilliant enough to cast a shadow on the sand. I used to stand there in wonderment and awe. The only sound that disturbed the stillness of the night and the sleeping patients was the barking of the dogs in the Arab city far away. This experience really impressed me and is one I should always remember.

It was towards the beginning of October that an Arab shepherd enquired why we remained in the cup-shaped depression which was our campsite, and when it was that we would be moving out. All of the area, we gathered, would be flooded to some depth when the rains came. Early one morning, as he led his flock of sheep past, he was perturbed to see us still there. To tell the truth, we thought that he wanted us to go because he believed we had relieved him of two of his sheep, which we had purchased at a very high price. This was the only meat we had had for some months, and the same applied to bread. So we asked him when the rains would come.

He answered, 'When you see a cloud as big as a man's hand come out of the horizon, then the rains will come and you must go quickly.'

Sure enough, the next morning, this really happened. The shepherd came running towards us, shouting, 'The cloud!! The cloud!!' as he pointed to a small cloud on the horizon, shaped like a man's hand.

Within two hours the sky was black. We got to work and dug wide and deep trenches around each tent, paying particular attention to the two wards. It was all to no avail, as by evening the rains came, heralded by winds so fierce we were compelled to look to our guy ropes, or our own tents would have been blown away. Truly I had never before seen the ferocity of a tropical rain storm, which was accompanied by forked lightning which ran along the ground like snakes. We awoke during the night to find the water had risen some 12 inches and most of us were suffering from wet clothes and bottoms.

At the first tinge of daylight the whole tented hospital managed to pull out with great difficulty, eventually arriving back at the dear old convent at Carthage for warmth, dry clothing and hot food.

Now when the Arab first mentioned the coming of the wet season he quoted unknowingly a story from the Old Testament. The actual story is to be found in the First Book of Kings, chapter 18, verses 42–45, and the incident in question relates to the wicked King Ahab and the prophet Elijah:

> So Ahab went to eat and drink. And Elijah went up to the top of Carmel he cast himself down upon the earth and put his face between his knees.
>
> He said to his servant go up now and look towards the sea and he went up and looked and said there is nothing. And he said go again seven times.
>
> And it came to pass that at the seventh time that he said behold the horizon there ariseth a little cloud out of the sea like a man's hand. And he said go up say unto Ahab, prepare by chariot and get thee down that the rain stop thee not. And it came to pass in the meanwhile that the heaven was black with clouds and wind and there was a great rain and Ahab rode and went into Jezreel.

Whilst at Kairouan we observed other biblical customs, such as the shepherds minding their flocks using slings and stones to protect their sheep and to recall strays, as did David the shepherd boy. Their aim was perfect, and when a truant was struck, the shepherd recalled it by name as one would a dog. It was a common sight to see a shepherd leading his flock and carrying a lamb on his shoulder. The women fetched the water from the well in stone jars, and these are then carried on their heads – it is not a task for men!

Arabs drink red wine, but I noticed that they always diluted it with water. I have seen camel drivers resting after bedding down their beasts and sipping their wine from earthenware bowls or cups under lean-to shelters made from palm fronds. I also noticed that they invariably flicked some water from a carafe onto the ground. When I enquired the reason for this, I was told that it was a gesture to express thanks to mother earth, whose needs were greater than man's. I personally think that it is a procedure to ensure that particles of dust and flies are removed. Looking back on this particular custom brings to mind the miracle of turning water into wine at Canaan of Galilee. This may be a possible explanation of an old tribal custom being adapted into the Gospels; if one has not sufficient wine for one's guests, I think that the most obvious thing to do is dilute it to make it to go further.

To help relieve the monotony and boredom among those patients confined to bed, we received a small portable gramophone complete with eight records, which were of the Edwardian era, songs such as 'Come into the Garden, Maude', etc. This gift came from one of the many societies dispensing comforts for the troops from London. Can you imagine how every time we had a new patient admitted he played the old repertoire over and over again? Finally, in sheer desperation, the records were smashed. Whilst the kindness of some dear old donor was fully appreciated, some of the gifts were somewhat incongruous. One of the patients received a hand-knitted balaclava helmet similar in colour to Joseph's famous coat of many colours. The recipient was suffering from malaria with a fluctuating temperature up to 106 degrees. I remember that it did make him smile, and that in itself was a rarity. There is little left to relate in regard to our short stay at Kairouan, except that in the October we had our busiest period in North Africa; we had admitted 210 patients to the hospital. The month before, it was 133. I think everyone was pleased to get away safely and return once more to Carthage.

The following poem was given to me by a young patient. I was not aware of the reason for this sudden inspiration; he simply was not that sort of chap. He made a rapid recovery after an appendectomy; perhaps it was the stifling heat of the tented ward. I remember it being around

100 degrees in the shade at the time. He certainly was not thinking of passing on. But the Cockney is noted for his ready wit and good humour; this was a typical example; but not the kind to reveal the higher thoughts that lie latent in most of us.

> Sat in those barren wastes,
> Where canvas serves to shield a skilful blade.
> Definitely each day the surgeon's hand is guided by God's aid,
> Ceaselessly healing tortured bodies wracked with pain through war,
> Like a mother with a weakly babe,
> Who knows no law other than to save.

The Jerboa

I have already mentioned this little rodent, commonly called the desert rat. They are mouse-like creatures about 6 to 8 inches tall, similar in size to a small squirrel. They have long rat-like tails tufted at the end and long hind legs; the front paws are quite small. They move in long leaps and in a zigzag fashion. Jerboas are commonly found in the African desert, particularly near to campsites where food is easily available. I think that it is their speed and sudden appearance which makes them so unpopular

I have in mind the following incident which is perhaps worthy of comment and which occurred near the tented hospital at Kairouan

It was a time when one of the nursing sisters was confined to her bed suffering from a mild attack of infective hepatitis jaundice – you may remember that in a previous chapter I mentioned our experience of this contagious disease while we were in Carthage. In this particular instance the patient was lying on a narrow camp bed in a small square tent with just a tarpaulin sheet to cover the ground. These conditions, together with the stifling heat (over 100 in the shade), did nothing to help combat the infection or give comfort to the patient.

It so happened that while she lay in her bed with half-closed eyes she suddenly became aware of a movement close by. Slowly turning her head, she was horrified to see just a few feet away the quizzical, beady eyes of a jerboa. She called softly to her batman, Joe, who was standing near the tent, to bring his gun and kill the intruder. He accordingly crawled silently in on all fours dragging his rifle and gently lifted the bottom of the canvas, whereupon he fired. Our little horror needed no warning and vanished with the speed of lightning, even before the shot came. Now whilst all this was happening a short distance away, the most important parade (pay parade) was in progress. The voice of the elderly Warrant Officer in charge resounded through the camp and even seemed to echo over the vast expanse of the desert. He was the usual type one meets as a 'regular', who no doubt had made the service his career from an early age. Of course, he was correctly attired in hat, shirt, shorts and polished shoes. As far as the rest of us were concerned, the days of spit and polish were long gone. Some of the chaps wore no shirts, just a pair of shorts and plimsoles! The men stood patiently waiting for their names to be called, then took two steps smartly forward to be identified by shouting the last three figures of their regimental number and name ('Smith 770!') and picked up their princely remuneration with a smart salute (senior officer also on parade). At this stage our friend the jerboa made a dash through the ranks straight under the trestle table and between the legs of the bawling Warrant Officer, who shouted,

'Someone shoot the *******!!!'

The pay table collapsed, scattering the documents, and worse still the cash which had been neatly stacked, all over the sand! The jerboa escaped fast enough, leaving behind a very embarrassed Warrant Officer endeavouring to readjust his shorts. I would not have been surprised if the jerboa was laughing his head off as he fled, as indeed all of the rest of us were . . . save for the aforesaid Warrant Officer.

The sequel to this was that the Warrant Officer wanted to know who the culprit was who had fired a shot without his permission. The frightened batman confessed, telling the Warrant Officer that he had acted on the orders of the sister. Thereupon the Warrant Officer stalked into the tent and told the sister that she could be put on a charge for ordering her batman to fire. He did not realise he had no authority to do this as the Princess Mary's Nursing Service was not at that time part of the RAF, and the sister told him so!

The Return to Carthage, and our First Christmas away from Home

After spending several months in the tented hospital at Kairouan in rather primitive conditions, and after that a short time at Le Bardo, where we were moved to on 7th November, it was back to Carthage.

We were indeed grateful to be back in the shelter of the convent exactly four weeks later. At first we had to endure the fierce wind of scorching heat which was the prelude to heavy rain, and this was followed by night frosts and light flurries of snow. Now, though – at last – we were dry.

During a period of changing duties I was transferred to the operating theatre. I had been invited by the monks (*the White Fathers*) to watch their night service and had promised to attend high mass at 2200 hours. However, on that particular night I was detailed to stand by in case of emergency. My duty expired, or should I say was supposed to expire, at midnight. An alarm came just before 2200 for all hospital staff to report for duty.

It appears that eight Army chaps had been celebrating in Tunis and had been staggering arm-in-arm along the main road to Carthage on their way back to camp. I believe that it was a French convoy of lorries and guns that scattered these poor devils, killing three outright and injuring the others. The hospital staff had to work flat out operating on the wounded and then attending to them in the wards. I reckon that the staff needed no reminders of that night. Hearing the clanging of the cathedral bells, the surgeon looked across the operating table and muttered miserably through his gauze mask, ''Appy Christmas'.

We eventually finished at 0400, just two hours before duty on the wards was due to start at 0600. What a Christmas Day! But thanks to our American friends we had everything one could wish for: turkey, pudding, fruit and nuts, not forgetting the drinks.

The hospital staff had collected palm fronds, which were then tied at the bottom of each bed, thus forming an archway down the centre of the wards. There was even a Christmas tree complete with a fairy made of cotton wool. In the evening there was an impromptu concert by the staff – I still have the printed menu and programme. Looking through this and seeing the various nicknames bought it all back. Ah, those happy days! It is still amusing to read the names of the artistes appearing in the programme:

'Laughing Boy' – who seldom smiled

'Mash and Tosh' – 'Inseparables', ex-male nurses from Repton [*sic, Rampton*] Mental Hospital

'Sweeney Todd' – male nurse

'Chunky' – male nurse

'We 3' – Doctors

'Jock Strap' – male nurse

'Lampedusa Kid' – male nurse

'Canterbury Killer' – 'Chippy', the coffin maker

These are only a few picked at random. It was a hilarious evening, and in spite of all the liquid refreshment nobody got drunk.

The party finished at 2200hrs, and we went back to normal duties the next day. However, at 1000 hours there was another emergency. A young Army chap during a fit of depression over Christmas 'committed the crime' (*suicide*), although I think this is a misnomer. This was a serious illness that had never been brought to our notice.

Now there is a sequel to this sad case. Soon after Christmas I wrote a letter home giving a full description of the festivities and a few details about how busy we had been. In the next letter from home I was told friends of ours at our respective offices had received the sad news of a relative having passed away in North Africa during the Christmas holidays. Their names were given, and I was able to inform them that the two young men died peacefully and without pain. They had the best of attention and were interred in the local cemetery with full military

THE RETURN TO CARTHAGE, AND OUR FIRST CHRISTMAS

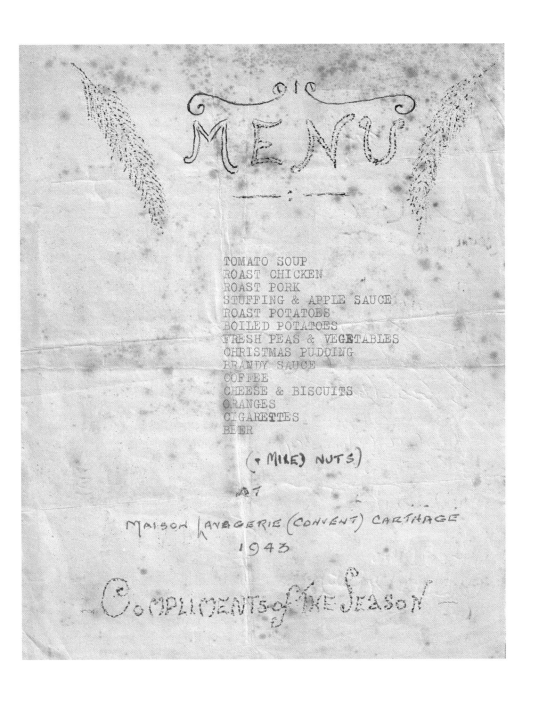

"HULLABULLOO"

by

"THE 31 MAD HATTER'S"

Straight from their greatest success "KAIROUAN KNIGHTS".

1. Opening Chorus by the Full Company.

2. The Famous Spanish Trio - Really Spanish - Straight from Spain.

3. Sketch -"MEAL TIMES IN THE COOKHOUSE" - by The Cookhouse Killer's - J. Stones and D. Maxfield.

4. Solo - The Famous Welsh Tenor - Nathanial Jones.

5. Sketch - "THE RETURN OF A SURGEON" - Featuring Geordie Redford, Canterbury Kell, Tillie Tindale, Ginger Maxfield and Smugger Smith.

6. Piano Solo - The Rippling Fingers of John Dennis Short.

7. Song - "THE LAMENT OF 31" - The Canterbury Killer & The Northern Knock-Out. Both artists secured at great expense ? ? ? ? 1 franc.

8. "A VOICE AND A PIANO" - By the Famous Northern Tenor Bill Tindale, and the Ivory King Len Burkinshaw.

INTERVAL

of 15 mins.

MUSIC BY KEN LOMAS ON THE PIANO.

THE RETURN TO CARTHAGE, AND OUR FIRST CHRISTMAS

"HULLABULLOO"
continued.

9. Solo - Ditties on the Piano - by The Famous Laughing Boy - Freddy Shotton.

10. Sketch - "EXPRESS SERVICE" - by Digger Lord and Tapper Hemming.

11. Rhythm - Big Bill Beaumont and his Harmonica Rascals.

12. "WE THREE" - by three of the lads - Duncan, Dinnick (M.O's) and Renson.

13. Comedy and Song - by The Northen Knock-Out - Geordie Redford.

14. Solo - "MUSIC FROM THE HIGHLANDS" - by Jock Murphy.

15. Sketch - "THE ORDEAL" - Featuring Freddy Shotton, Harry Keen and Smugger Smith.

16. Finale - "WHEN DAY IS DONE" By the Full Company.

Compere - Digger Lord.

Produced by the Company.

Stage Manager - "THE LAMPEDUSA KID" - Denny Gurney.

Lighting Effects by "SPARKS" Murphy and his Oil-Rag Bill Beaumont.

Scene Shifters and Prop Men - Anybody thats willing.

NURSING AT THE FRONTLINE

THE RETURN TO CARTHAGE, AND OUR FIRST CHRISTMAS

honours. This seems stranger than fiction all those miles away and these two chaps were among those we had dealt with on Christmas Eve.

I believe that Scra changed a few details here, as the CWGC appears not to have any records of these chaps. The only ones they have for this date are buried in Algiers, 515 miles from this location!

One day not long after Christmas, one of the Medical Officers, a Dr Dinnick, asked if I had ever done a PM (post mortem), I replied in the negative.

'Care to join me?' he asked. 'Bring plenty of cigarettes with you.'

On the way to the room which was used as a mortuary he told me the facts of the case. It appeared that two friends had gone into town on the spree. On the way home, having had sufficient hooch, they became – shall we say? – 'playful' and started pushing each other about. Unfortunately, one of them fell and struck his head, which proved fatal. The body was brought into the hospital, and the companion was held under open arrest until the cause of death was determined.

I shall not describe the process in detail except to say that it was not unlike the situation in which one has just bought a new car and lifted up the bonnet with the instruction manual at hand. Ah, one might say, there are the plugs, and that is the carburettor. That was exactly my reaction when the chest wall was removed; nothing gruesome about that. However, I am glad to say the findings proved it to be a case of accidental death.

The surgeon left after completing the procedure, leaving me to attend to the preparations for committal. His parting action was to ring the orderly room and tell them to send two GD (Ground Staff) for menial tasks to clean the room. That meant mopping up the marble floor. I had completed my part by the time I heard two Cockneys coming down the long corridor dragging their brooms and clanking their galvanised buckets, the conversation including a choice selection of adjectives. The necessary instructions were given, including a warning not to move or touch the body, which lay on the marble topped table suitably covered with a white sheet.

'I'll send Chippy up with the coffin later', I said, then left them to their task amid protestations and proceeded down the corridor.

I had just reached the staircase when I heard an ear-piercing yell and saw two bedraggled men running for their lives.

'What the devil is wrong with you two?' I asked

'You told us he was dead!' they replied.

'Of course he is', said I.

'Well, as we were washing the floor, but the body made a noise . . . ugh!'

I had quite a job convincing them that it was only a pocket of air escaping from the corpse. The air must have been very blue!

> *The surgeon who invited Scra to the post mortem was Dr Oswald Peter Dinnick, MB, BS, MRCS, LRCP, DA, RAF No.117969, who had trained at University College London and the Middlesex Hospital Medical School. His first appointment in 1939 was as a Resident Casualty Officer 'with other duties' – a wartime title at the Middlesex. He remained there for two years as an anaesthetist. After this he spent four years in the Royal Air Force and reached the rank of Squadron Leader.*
>
> *After the war, 'OPD' – as he was affectionately known – returned to the Middlesex, remaining as consultant there until 1982. He spoke and published widely and was variously Secretary, Vice President, and President of several anaesthetic societies and a founder member of the History of Anaesthesia Society. He died in September 1995.*

Whilst at Carthage I was detailed to visit a radar unit some miles south of Tunis towards Kasserine called El Jem. The object of the mission was to ascertain whether they had received their quota of inoculations. The driver of the Jeep and I left the hospital very early in the morning to enable us to reach this outpost well before the midday heat. We had been travelling for about three hours through rough desert terrain without meeting any one, and to tell the truth I was getting rather anxious, fearing that we had taken the wrong track. However we found a donkey's shoe which rather comforted us, and later on we saw the tracks of a camel.

Quite suddenly I spotted a white building in the distance, and we decided to pull up and rest in the shade for a while. When we came closer we discovered that it was a small Roman circus or colosseum in a perfect state of preservation. It was uncanny – it seemed to us as though the people or spectators had only just left.

Now, I must admit that anything historic is something that I cannot resist, but unfortunately my driver was not the least bit interested. We sat in the shade of an archway leading into the arena and enjoyed a short rest and refreshment. Before we resumed our journey I decided to explore the remainder of the chambers and eventually found a cave.

'What a smell of cats', commented the driver. 'I suppose you are going to tell me it's the lions' den.'

While he was talking I happened to look up at the roof of the cavern and observed a line of small holes about half an inch in diameter stretching across the entrance.

I said, 'Yes, I think that this was connected with the animals of the period.'

'Come off it, I'm not barmy enough to believe that', he replied.

I then pointed to the holes in the ceiling and persuaded him to help scoop away the sand on the floor to see if there were holes corresponding with those above, and to my amazement we found them. But my companion was not convinced.

'Do you mean to say that what we can smell was made by the lions centuries ago?' he asked.

I had to do some quick thinking.

'What does a dog do when you take him out for a walk? I think the explanation is that the animals of the desert have sheltered here at night for centuries past and still do.'

We finally found the outpost of army technicians, six in all, perfectly fit and well but terribly lonely. We stayed with them for about an hour and then left as we were anxious to get back to base before dark. We did have a picture taken before we left. The cameraman told us to stick out our chests, hence the rather 'Tarzan' look to us!

> *This site was known to the Romans as Thysdrus. The museums at El Djem consist of the amphitheatre, a reconstructed Roman villa and the museum. There are large numbers of excellent mosaics, and you can still wander around the site at will. It scores very highly on TripAdvisor.*

At the desert outpost.

I must now tell you about an important event during our stay in Carthage. The hospital had been functioning for nearly a year at Maison Lavigerie, and during that time the bedstate varied from about 50 patients to over 400. We had a dental clinic run by an efficient dental surgeon and staff, a 'Path Lab' commonly known by all as 'Bugs', and a fully equipped operating theatre.

It is pretty certain that the word 'epidemic' caused some apprehension among the personnel, for it meant long and exhausting hours of intensive care and attention for all sections. Yes, we had received the message all right, there was an epidemic of infective hepatitis, commonly known as jaundice. It was a killer and infectious. The numbers mounted daily, and to make our work harder and more difficult our surgical ward was full, thus compelling us to use every available space for beds, even putting stretcher cases in the corridors. Shift duty was out of the question; we were working from 0600 hrs to 2300 hrs with no rest days. We simply could not carry on like this for long. It meant we were unable to attend to our own needs, such as washing our clothes. However, we did manage a personal wash down before getting into bed. As far as I can recall, we had three deaths from jaundice and several others after surgery.

Among the nursing staff was a young boy, a Scot aged nineteen, who contracted the disease, a condition of inflammation of the liver. We saw that he had every sign and symptom and advised him to report sick. This he refused to do, realising that by doing so he would add to the burden being carried by his friends. He eventually collapsed and passed away, a fine example of devotion to his duty to his patients which is still remembered by those of us who are left.

The treatment for this disease was a completely fat-free diet. All that we could provide was tinned salmon, bread – if available – biscuits (hard tack), meat and veg (tinned) and porridge (crushed biscuits in water). In some less serious cases we risked a variation by including a very small portion of cheese plus tea without milk.

A sequel to this, but in a lighter vein, was an incident depicting relaxation during a difficult and trying period. One evening, we found that there was insufficient room in a small square mortuary tent for six bodies; the tent would only hold three. Here was a dilemma for us nurses. A solution had to be found, but what? The hospital itself boasted a large reception room. The duty corporal was a Cockney who always volunteered for night duty. Very few admissions were made between 2200 and 0800, so he always had the opportunity of a few hours' sleep, thus leaving the following day free for him to go into town.

We had earlier, after our arrival in Carthage, held a small and polite – although formal protest against the long hours actually on duty. These hours had been modified, and as a special concession the nursing staff were allowed four hours' rest between 1400 hrs and 1800 hrs, on condition that only one person was absent from the ward at any one time.

Talking among ourselves during the afternoon, it was suggested that we wrap the bodies in a blanket on a board and then stand them up in the long stationery cupboard – which had large sliding doors – in reception until morning, doing this before the corporal came on duty at 2200. The day staff came off duty at that time, and the only exit from the hospital was through reception. When the hour came, we trooped out, passing a fond farewell to the corporal but also threatening to beat him up if he admitted any more patients during the night. Arriving on duty the next morning, we enquired from the corporal (whom we called 'Tubby') if he had a quiet night and if he had made any admissions? He replied in the negative.

'Did you sleep most of the night?'

'Well, did I hell!' he replied. 'Bloody awful smell of dead bodies kept me awake.'

'Oh sorry, Tubby, we forgot to tell you about those in the cupboard. We have come in early to remove them for burial straight away.'

There was no disrespect to the deceased

✚

On to Italy

Most of the units of both Army and Air Force had advanced into Sicily and then forward to the mainland; consequently, the number of patients declined. Postings were coming through pretty fast, and it all sounded so ominous. Naturally, the staff became apprehensive about the future and they felt the breaking-up like the parting of old friends

After a few months in winter quarters, only using the smaller rooms of the convent as wards, we looked forward to an early spring. It was about the beginning of February when we observed a rise in temperature and noticed a tinge of colour among the ruins, where some wild flowers were lifting their heads towards the sun. Yes, spring had arrived, and our morale began to rise when we were told we were on the move again.

Nursing Orderlies, 31 MFH, 25th March 1944.

Now it was really goodbye to Carthage. Our destination wasn't so far away this time. We closed the hospital on 5th March 1944 and were told to stand by, ready to proceed to an embarkation area.

After almost a month patiently waiting for the day of embarkation, a merchant ship became available to transport us to Italy. This vessel could only accommodate our unit, and with all the vehicles aboard very little space was left for us to sleep comfortably. The majority of us rested on the open deck.

On 2nd April we arrived at the Tunisian port of Bizerte and were sent to the Texas Transit Camp outside the town, camping temporarily in the long, lush grass. How it was refreshing to smell the sweetness of freshly trodden turf. This was the first time since we left England that we had seen grass. That was eleven months ago. We felt elated; at least we were now on the right track towards home.

We slipped quietly away at nightfall on a warm clear night, steaming slowly through calm waters and keeping well into the coastline. It was no hardship to sleep on deck; in fact, it was far more pleasant than below.

No escort, no lights, no smoking, and above all else keep your voices down: all these precautions were necessary as enemy U-Boats were always a potential danger. We had already experienced an attack upon our convoy on the way out from England to Algiers. This had been a frightening ordeal, trapped down on F deck below the waterline. Two ships were sunk, with only a few survivors. It was also another reason to sleep on deck. This was one of many incidents which are best forgotten. Now we were once again at the mercy of the U-Boats in the Mediterranean.

> *Scra has I believe, 'glossed over' quite a number of incidents, and a number of others have been amalgamated, quite possibly for his own sake. This probably explains the difficulty I have had in tracing individual deaths and personnel from the unit.*

To proceed with our journey . . . we kept close to the Sicilian coast, passing Palermo and Messina. We then took a diagonal route towards the Gulf of Eufemia on the Italian mainland. Here was a spectacle that we would have missed had we been below decks. There was on the horizon a sky ablaze – we could see an eruption of the active volcano, Stromboli.

> *Stromboli is a small island in the Tyrrhenian Sea, off the north coast of Sicily, containing one of the four active volcanoes in Italy. It has been in continuous eruption of varying degrees, it is estimated, for the past two to five thousand years. Although in the period from 1930 to 1939 the explosive eruptions are very well documented, those from 1940 to the early 1950s are not at all. This is for quite obvious reasons.*

It reminded us so much of Guy Fawkes Night. The volcano resembled a dark cone with gigantic boulders and a cascade of hot debris being shot high into the air, and streams of glowing lava snaking their way down the slopes into a sizzling sea. This was an awe-inspiring sight, and I doubt we will ever see its like again.

At daybreak we arrived at the port of Torre Annunziata, near Naples. We realised it would take practically the whole day to unload our gear, so it was decided to land the Bedford lorries first, each containing the necessary rations and most of the staff to convey us up to an assembly point a few miles away at Portici. Here we were told to wait for the remainder of the cargo.

The assembled convoy would then depart for our final destination through the precipitous Apennine Mountains to the Adriatic coast. In the meantime, permission had been given for us to take a few hours of

Outside Portici, the assembly area.

freedom on condition that everyone was back at the assembly point by 1630 hrs, as the convoy would leave promptly at 1700 hrs. Fortunately, I was aware that the famous ruins of Pompeii were in the vicinity and I realised that a golden opportunity lay before me. I somehow felt that I might not pass this way again; nor did I.

The main autostrada lay close by, so I was able to thumb a lift, which was comparatively easy as there was a steady stream of army trucks going to and fro taking supplies to the advancing troops.

The journey did not take too long – there was no speed limit that day as far as the army were concerned. On the way two young Army chaps jumped on, quite the polite and educated type! They seemed to be well acquainted with the history of Pompeii. The truck halted outside the entrance to the ancient site. The place seemed to be deserted except for an aged attendant who eagerly extended his hand for the admission fee. We three walked slowly through the silent streets, pausing from time to time to consult the guide book. There was so much to see and absorb in such a short time.

Now before I mention just a few historical notes, I should say that Pompeii resembled a blitzed city, but without the rubble and dust. Streets in systematic lines were paved with huge blocks of flat stone and had a raised pavement on either side. At intervals, stepping stones were placed which enabled people to cross the road during any period of torrential

Above and opposite: *Two views of Vesuvius from Naples, and two pictures of a very quiet Pompeii.*

ON TO ITALY

rain, and these were so spaced to allow chariots or carts to pass. All the rainwater flowed into the deep gutters, which carried it away to specially constructed underground cisterns, this being the only source of water for drinking and domestic use.

The principal site is the forum. This was the civic centre around which revolved the everyday life of the citizens. It is rectangular and measures 515 feet long and 107 feet wide, with tall marble columns around the perimeter. The huge temples of Venus, Jupiter and Apollo were situated in the area, and from what remained standing one gained the impression of the skilful planning which was used so many centuries ago.

Other buildings which had been excavated and renovated over the years included an open covered theatre, the barracks of the gladiators, the amphitheatre, and the tepidarium of the bath house, all of which were very well preserved.

One must not forget the wonderfully painted interior walls in the houses of the rich patricians and the various kinds of shops. These are alive with the colours of the past, and a dinner in one of these opulent houses can be easily imagined, with the painted walls and tessellated mosaic floors showing the high status of the individuals who lived and most likely died there.

The buildings are truly an impressive sight against the dark, brooding and forbidding backcloth of Vesuvius, which intensified the desolation. Who knows when this mountain would erupt again, and who would be captured by the devastating flows next time?

> *Vesuvius erupted on 17 March 1944, the eruption lasting for a week and a half. Luckily, there was a fast and effective response from the Allied forces in the area who assisted in the rescue and clear-up operations. The USAAF did lose 88 B-25 Mitchell Bombers of the reputedly unlucky 340th Bomb Group, at an estimated cost of $25 million. The group was later made famous by the 1961 book* Catch 22, *written by an actual member of the unit, Joseph Heller. Thankfully, Vesuvius, although still a very active volcano, has not erupted since that date*

All the events in the life of the city had been recorded in the walls and some of the graffiti told more of the human side of life – for instance,

ON TO ITALY

the innkeeper had tabulated the debts due to him. There were business appointments and even messages from lovers, all beautifully written. Upon one wall the alphabet was inscribed to teach children. Caricatures and obscene drawings were particularly found on the 'houses of ill repute'.

These are but a few items of special interest picked at random from my old guide book, which I have had to refer to from time to time. I notice the date faintly visible inside the cover (1944), a long time in which to remember so much detail.

> *It is to be noted that Scra made notes in his guide book, especially one to be aware of pickpockets, but looking at the pictures he took in 1944, it appears he and his chums were the only visitors that day. It was certainly packed out when I last visited!*

Now after we had taken a very rapid tour, keeping our eyes on the clock all the time, we found that we had become so absorbed that we'd completely forgotten to eat so we had to call it a day.

Within a few yards of the entrance we observed a very pretty beer garden with gaily coloured umbrellas. We were offered a roll of bread, plus a large glass of champagne, all for 5 lire. (*In 1943 the exchange rate for Italian lire to sterling was 480 to the pound, so 5 lire translates as around 2d in pre-decimal money, which is less than 1p today, even allowing for inflation!*) The cheapest lunch I have ever had. We managed to arrive back in time for a wash and brush-up. I found my allotted place in the convoy and away we went, dead on time.

Now let's see what Bari, our next destination, had to offer

Bari

After we left Naples, the convoy proceeded on yet another journey The route took us through the picturesque Italian countryside, giving us the opportunity of seeing for the first time the beauty of the verdant pastoral scenery so very different from the scorching plains of North Africa.

So we gradually climbed through the foothills, passing the quaint villages, each one dominated by its church, that lie between places which had become prominent during the war such as Caserta, Benevento and Ariano.

Caserta had been devastated, and not many buildings remained intact as we passed to the next town, Benevento. This small town and the area around were noted for many vineyards which produced excellent wines.

Some months later, I returned to visit a farm on the outskirts for the sole purpose of buying two or more 10-gallon drums of the famous local brew, Vermouth. I think we paid 5 lire a pint! I was at that time stationed with 73 (Spitfire) Squadron near Termoli. Our so-called canteen resold this potent vintage for 10 lire a pint; the profit was passed to our comforts fund, part of which purchased such luxuries as fruit, eggs, meat, etc. to supplement our meagre rations; additionally, we bought live chickens and a goose. If memory serves, I believe we also acquired a piglet, plus a pet or two – a caged bird, a cat, and a dog.

So when the squadron was on the move it was quite a comical sight, with the various wooden cases perched high on the lorries. It resembled a travelling circus rather than a squadron going into action. To revert to the Vermouth vino, this was sold on condition that the consumer was limited to three pints only, as after the fourth pint a chap would be out for 24 hours. Needless to say, the NAAFI beer was in short supply and other imported brands seemed of poor quality. I am sorry to slightly

BARI

Above and below: *Typical Italian villages on the way to Bari.*

deviate, and I shall comment more fully in another chapter. (*See 'Spitfire Squadron'*)

To continue . . . the climb gradually became steeper as we approached the Apennine mountain range, often referred to as the backbone of Italy. We progressed slowly through the enveloping mist. It was very dense at times; we could hear the sound of the bells around the necks of the grazing cattle which roamed these parts, but seldom saw them.

The atmosphere was cold, damp and murky. In fact, at times it sent shivers down your spine. Ariano, as we approached it, resembled a cluster of stone huts, each of which usually accommodated a family – mother, father, several children, the chickens and sometimes the cow, all in one room. It was all so primitive. Outside the door was a charcoal fire over which stood the tripod and traditional cooking pot. This appeared to be the only source of heating. I should imagine that conditions in severe weather, particularly in the winter, would have been grim and desolate.

Ariano was the scene of some very severe fighting. The number of casualties must have been extremely heavy in this wild terrain.

As we descended the slopes, the mist gradually cleared, it became noticeably warmer and we could see cultivated fields before us. From then on it was a fairly straight run to the Adriatic coast and Barletta.

Proceeding along with the warm sea breezes, we passed through San Spirito – quite a small fishing village on the outskirts of the modern town of Bari. Here we halted (near the Eighth Army rest camp) outside a long narrow building which had been a school. It contained several larger rooms as wards, and a smaller one as a private ward for the officers.

It was here at Bari that we were transferred to the newly formed Balkan Air Force in June 1944.

> *The Balkan Air Force (BAF) was formed in response to the changing and indeed growing importance of the Balkans, which included the sea east of Italy, Yugoslavia and Greece. This newly formed Allied air force, comprising both British and American squadrons, was allocated six airfields in Italy and an advanced control, command and landing strip at Vis. Thus, to deal with the high number of Allied and especially Partisan casualties, 31 MFH at Bari Airport took charge of coordinating, receiving and evacuation of casualties by air to Bari.*

In spite of all this space, our initial intake of patients was not large and not of special interest. Moreover, the majority of the patients were for recuperation and medical aftercare.

BARI

Bari Old Town, 1944.

Of course we were still a fully equipped hospital – operating theatre, path lab, X-Ray department, etc. – but we did not have the number of patients we had been accustomed to whilst at Carthage.

Not long after we arrived at Bari, two young Italian girls volunteered to assist us with the nursing care on the wards. Both came from very good local families. They received no payment, but in lieu of monetary remuneration we provided accommodation, food and a uniform. The major problem was that neither of them spoke any English! However, as I was the senior member of ward staff, they came under my protection. It was amazing how quickly we got along, and how famously we did get along, with my limited Italian and inevitable gestures. We soon came to understand each other very well.

Above and below: *31MFH at Bari.*

The building was, before the war, a girls' school with its own beach for swimming, the San Francesco all'Arena School in Fesca, a suburb of Bari. Sadly, it has now been demolished.

I had been delegated for a while to be in charge of the officers' ward consisting of ten beds. I enjoyed this duty as very few medical treatments were necessary, so I had time to relax and chat with the inmates, from the lowly pilot officer to those of much higher rank.

In a ward full of these types no special recognition of rank was observed. They were all patients to me, although they were all treated with the utmost respect. I believe they preferred it that way, but even a hospital has its military regulations and discipline which must be observed by both patients and staff.

My duties commenced at 0800 hrs daily, and I never returned to my sleeping quarters until late in the evening, but that was of my own choice.

Each evening, we had the opportunity of enjoying discussions on all sorts of subjects, which inspired one to serious thinking. There was only one unpleasant incident; it happened one night during a convivial chat.

A young officer interrupted the conversation by shouting, 'What time is supper? I'm hungry!'

Immediately, the others demanded the same.

The Italian Nursing Assistants at Bari, Scra on the right.

'We want bread cheese and onions, and don't forget our extra ration of Guinness!'

I was dumbfounded and tried to convince them that it was quite impossible to produce any kind of food at that time of night – in any case, the kitchen was locked. It was then suggested by a senior officer that I should obtain the key from the orderly room and procure whatever was required. This 'suggestion' I flatly refused to agree to, reminding them that they had had a pretty good meal a couple of hours earlier and I was not willing to risk the chance of finding myself on a 'fizzer'.

> *A fizzer means being bought before a senior officer and charged with 'misconduct', which can have a very broad application. It would normally resemble a small magistrates' court, in which the senior officer acts as judge and jury weighing up evidence, with a senior non-commissioned officer – normally the Station Warrant Officer in the RAF or his equivalent in the Army – as a witness, handing down a sentence, or 'award' as it is described in military parlance. The final words, usually, are:*
>
> *'Do you accept my award?'*
>
> *A wise answer would be, 'Yes, sir.'*
>
> *The option of taking your case to 'higher authority' or Courts Martial are always deemed a gamble too far, and the 'award' of being confined to barracks or a fine – or sometimes both – is handed down amid sighs all round. For repeat miscreants and serial offenders, time in military jail is often an option. An educational 'talk' then follows!*

However, the officer who asked me to get the key undertook full responsibility and furthermore suggested that I should be accompanied by two officers to assist in carrying such a large and varied supply. Would I then obey the order? Well, this was agreed upon, and I can still see the face of the orderly Sergeant when the kitchen key was requested! However, he was not in a position to refuse. We managed to carry back two large loaves, a hunk of cheese, several large onions and twenty-four bottles of beer. Later that night, it became a rip-roaring binge before finally reaching the stage of a grand pillow fight. The ward was a shambles – feathers everywhere, with food and empty beer bottles rolling around the floor.

That was the limit, I'm afraid! I protested in pretty strong words, telling them, 'You may wallow in this mess, but I shall refuse to clean the place up in the morning', and walked out.

I did not arrive so punctually the next morning and I was certainly not looking forward to my reception. Taking courage, I pushed wide the swing doors and stood astounded.

'Morning, Harry!' came the chorus, but no, it was not the friendly greeting that shook me . . . The whole ward was back to normal – not a feather to be seen, not a thing out of place. The floor had been swept and washed, beds made, and there was a wide grin on all their faces. The originator of the escapade came forward with profuse apologies for all the mischief and unruly behaviour.

Looking back, they were a grand bunch of chaps in spite of their gold braid and schoolboy pranks – even the Wing Commander Padre, who literally threw away his dog collar that evening.

You know, there are times when memories make you feel good and wish you were young again. I was destined to meet that Padre again under different circumstances, but that's another story we shall follow later. The following tribute was composed by one of these officer patients and given to me the day he left hospital.

Reflections under treatment

The sprightly Scra, so keen intense,
Is deadly with his instruments.
With axe so keen chops off a toe,
You really do not see it go!
So swiftly wielded in its flight,
Followed up with knife so bright,
Carving patterns on the soles –
Excavating mighty holes.
When I get out I hope to seek
No more his torturing technique.

with gratitude and good wishes
F.C. Dench F/Lt
October 1944

Background to Bari, Partisans and the SOE Mission to Yugoslavia

The Kingdom of the Serbs, Croats and Slovenes was created in 1918 after the Great War and the break-up of the Austro-Hungarian Empire, and it became the Kingdom of Yugoslavia in October 1929.

The Second World War came to the country on 6 April 1941, when German, Italian and Hungarian forces invaded. After eleven days an armistice was signed.

Yugoslavia was then split into almost its constituent pre-1918 parts (Serbia, Montenegro, State of Slovenes Croats and Serbs, Fiume, and the ceded parts of Austria-Hungary), with Croatia becoming a Nazi puppet state ruled over by a fascist organization called the Ustaše.

The Balkans have always been a 'bête noire' for armies due to the number of different ethnic and religious identities in the area. It is also named in one of the three cardinal rules of the teachings of the Royal Military Academy, Sandhurst:

> *Never advance on Moscow.*
> *Never make advances to the Colonel's daughter.*
> *And most importantly . . . Never make war in the Balkans.*

After the German invasion, two groups of resistance partisans sprang up, the communists under Jozef Broz (later known as Marshal Tito), and the initially royalist group the 'Chetniks' (a name that would resonate into the 1990s) led by Draža Mihajlović. The Chetniks would soon focus on opposing the communist partisans and would also persecute and kill Muslims and Croats, soon collaborating with the Nazis.

The Ustaše themselves in return persecuted the Serbs, Jews and Romany peoples of the Balkans, killing around 300,000 Serbs and 30,000 Jews and Romany.

The history of the Balkans and its wars and border changes warrants a book in itself. Suffice to say that the 1990s Bosnian war which formally ended with the Dayton agreement of 1995 was also full of atrocities. In fact, the Ustaše themselves were so vicious that the Gestapo wrote a report to Himmler, the head of the SS, in February 1942 stating:

> *Increased activity of the bands [partisans] is chiefly due to the atrocities carried out by the Ustaše units in Croatia . . . The Ustaše committed their deeds in a bestial manner, not only against males of conscript age, but especially against helpless old people, women, and children. The number of the Orthodox that the Ustaše have massacred and sadistically tortured to death is around 300,000.*

If the Gestapo called the atrocities 'bestial' and spoke of people 'sadistically tortured to death', the crimes committed must have been appalling.

Suffice to say, the Allies threw in their lot with Tito and began to supply arms and aid to the partisans after a series of territorial gains against the Germans. This was supported by the Special Operations Executive (SOE), and the first mission, Operation Typical, was led by William Deakin, who met up with Tito himself. His reports are thought to have had an enormous impact on British policy in the Balkans and support of the partisans.

Brigadier Fitzroy Maclean led the second operation, and it was he who initiated 'Mission Rogers', in which Major Lindsay Rogers and his initial team of three led a daring mission (the British Medical Mission) deep into enemy territory. Working under enormous difficulties, and relying solely upon air drops to fulfil their needs, they built a makeshift operating theatre from corrugated iron and rough wood and achieved remarkable results. It was said at the time that a surgeon was more valuable to the partisans than a whole division. Supplies were dropped by the newly formed Balkan Air Force. These drops included food, medical aid and clothing, as well as arms and ammunition.

They were dropped onto pre-arranged locations and more often than not at sites hidden in forest clearings or villages far into the snow-covered mountains.

Many of the wounded, and civilians too, were in a desperate state and required urgent medical intervention even after the good offices of Major Rogers and his team. This is where the air evacuations came in and when Scra first encountered the partisans. It was not to be his last encounter by any means . . .

Reception of Partisan Refugees at Bari

I still have in my possession the copy of 'Standing Orders' which I received that gave me the full details of this important mission.

I think it is now perfectly safe to disclose the contents of the order relating to this operation. Written across the top of the paper is the word 'Secret' in large red letters, and it is dated May 16th 1944.

This order was distributed in the morning of the 16th whilst we were engaged upon our normal duties.

The canopy of the night sky was dark, with masses of cloud formations drifting slowly across the nearby airfield at Bari which was empty save for a small building, the control centre, away in the corner. It was simply a large field, devoid of runways or anything that would suggest its purpose.

This then was the secret rendezvous. We arrived by ambulance with the truck at the appointed hour of 2300 hours.

A Bedford lorry had preceded us a couple of hours earlier loaded with the heavy equipment for large marquee tents, several ridge tents, cookhouse utensils – including two large 'Soyer' boilers which can be either large cookers or hold huge amounts of tea or coffee – trestle tables and blankets, together with the usual medical – or should I say hygienic – receptacles.

By the time we arrived most of the sections had been assembled and tents had been erected on the site close to the road exit; this would facilitate a quick and effective dispatch of the many ambulances to the base hospitals.

Only a few oil lamps were placed at strategic points. One hurricane lamp hung inside each of the large reception tents. Other than that it was a complete blackout to prevent detection by enemy aircraft.

SECRET

DC3s ARRIVAL FROM
11 p/c TO DAWN (50/c)

TO
AIRFIELD RECEPTION
AT BARI - ITALY

STANDING ORDERS

FOR THE AIR EVACUATION SECTION OF NO. 31 M.F.H.

The following personnel will work as a "team" in order to dispose of patients evacuated by air in the most efficient and expeditious manner possible. All personnel will act as Stretcher Bearers with the exception of Cookhouse personnel. The loading and unloading of aircraft and/or ambulances should at all times be carried out as quickly as possible, with the minimum of discomfort to the patients.

The following instructions are issued as a guide to all personnel concerned. If these instructions are carried out conscientiously, the work will be made easier for all concerned, and the safe custody of all equipment ensured.

SGT. KIRKBRIDE. General supervision - notifying staff of time of "take off" - accommodation of patients - compiling of register - compilation of return for C.O's signature - collection and safe custody of D.D's - ensuring quick "turn-about" during unloading of ambulances at tented site - cleaning up of tented site on completion of operations.

SGT. LEYLAND. - i/c Tentage - to ensure quick and efficient loading of Ambulances from aircraft.

CPL. HAY - To ensure that TWO Surgical Haversacks, and supplies of Cotton Wool, Bandages, Aspirin, Codeine, etc. are placed on board 3 Ton Bedford. N.C.O. i/c NO. 1 Ambulance.

CPL. HILL - To ensure that telephone, Bed Pan, Urinal and Tow is placed on board 3 Ton Bedford. N.C.O. i/c No. 2 Ambulance.

LAC. WRIGHT and LAC. LESLIE - No. 1 Ambulance.

LAC. SCRAFIELD and LAC. SMITH - No. 2 Ambulance.

LAC. SMITH - To ensure that Latrine Buckets, Lids and paper are placed on board Bedford. Supervise emptying of latrine buckets by R.A.F. sanitary squad on completion of night duty.

LAC. HANMER and AC. CLAYTON - Cooking and distribution of food and refreshments to patients. Erection and clearing up of cookhouse site.

AC. BUMPHREY - To assist in erection and clearing of Cookhouse Site. To assist SGT. LEYLAND with unloading of aircraft.

LAC. KEITH - Driver No. 1 Ambulance. To act as Stretcher Bearer.

LAC. CANNING Driver No. 2 Ambulance. To act as Stretcher Bearer.

LAC. BUTLER Driver 3 Ton Bedford (walking cases). To assist in unloading of aircraft.

LAC. ALDRED Driver of Thorneycroft. To ensure vehicle is loaded with adequate supply of Stretchers and Blankets before leaving hospital. To assist in unloading of aircraft.

LAC. COX - Driver of Bedford conveying Cookhouse. To ensure that vehicle is outside Ration Stores in time for rations and utensils to be loaded prior to departure. To assist

Above and opposite: *The secret standing orders.*

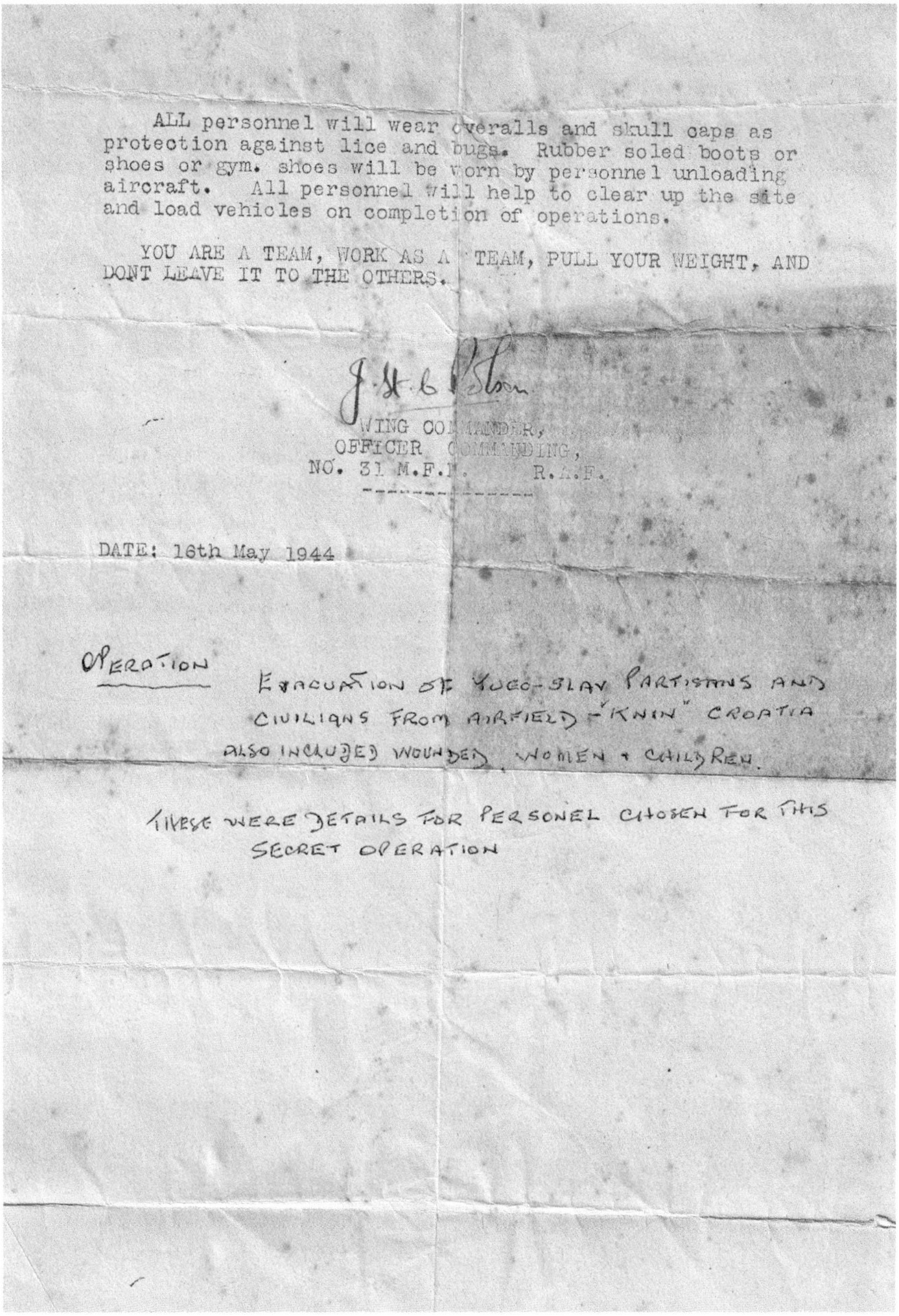

RECEPTION OF PARTISAN REFUGEES AT BARI

ALL personnel will wear overalls and skull caps as protection against lice and bugs. Rubber soled boots or shoes or gym. shoes will be worn by personnel unloading aircraft. All personnel will help to clear up the site and load vehicles on completion of operations.

YOU ARE A TEAM, WORK AS A TEAM, PULL YOUR WEIGHT, AND DONT LEAVE IT TO THE OTHERS.

[signature]

WING COMMANDER,
OFFICER COMMANDING,
NO. 31 M.F.U.   R.A.F.

DATE: 16th May 1944

OPERATION EVACUATION OF YUGO-SLAV PARTISANS AND CIVILIANS FROM AIRFIELD - "KNIN" CROATIA ALSO INCLUDED WOUNDED, WOMEN + CHILDREN.

THESE WERE DETAILS FOR PERSONEL CHOSEN FOR THIS SECRET OPERATION

Midnight came as we waited in silence for the sound of an approaching plane. This would be the signal for guiding lights to be placed at intervals to assist the pilots to the nearest point of the reception area. This was the most important part of the operation, as speedy unloading was imperative both for the patients and for the dispersal of the empty aeroplane to its allotted parking space.

When the first plane came low at 0100 hrs it circled and then made a smooth landing.

As soon as the door swung open, the truck containing the doctors raced out, followed by the ambulance and lorry. We clambered up into the plane with difficulty, carefully avoiding treading upon the occupants on the crowded floor. We shepherded those able to walk down out of the plane into the lorry, thus providing enough space for us to use the stretchers and carry out the others to the nearest tent.

We could not segregate the many types of cases at that point. There was practically every kind of condition: gunshot wounds, traumatic amputations of limbs, medical cases including several suffering from TB and bronchitis – men, women and children all in a deplorable condition. It was impossible to attend to their immediate needs as more planes were circling the airfield patiently awaiting the signal to land. Our immediate task was to carry them in and lay them on the ground in the tents as close together as possible; those able to walk were sat in groups.

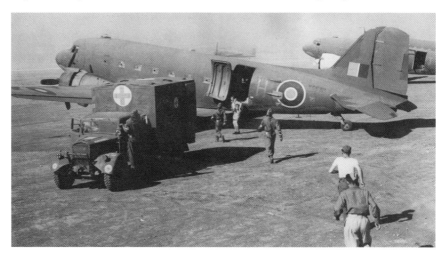

Air ambulance, and arrival of patients. Note the wearing of 'Typhus Suits' to prevent contagion.

RECEPTION OF PARTISAN REFUGEES AT BARI

After the landing of the first three planes there was a welcome interval before the arrival of the next load. This gave us the opportunity to hand round refreshments: tinned chicken sandwiches and hot coffee, and hot milk to the children.

In between times, frequent calls were made . . . '*Zac-cot, Druge!!*' ('Bed pan, comrade!!'). We had so many requests that it became impossible to cope with the demand. The male urinals were passed one to another and then dumped upon the ground until we found time to dispose of the contents.

RECEPTION OF PARTISAN REFUGEES AT BARI

NURSING AT THE FRONTLINE

RECEPTION OF PARTISAN REFUGEES AT BARI

NURSING AT THE FRONTLINE

RECEPTION OF PARTISAN REFUGEES AT BARI

NURSING AT THE FRONTLINE

RECEPTION OF PARTISAN REFUGEES AT BARI

I remember one such incident during another night clambering over the patients endeavouring to cope with the demand. A cry came from the far end – '*Zac–cot, Druge!!*'

I grabbed a urinal and thrust it into the hand of the sufferer. This was the signal for a burst of laughter from everyone. In my haste to oblige, I had tripped and only just managed to remain vertical. I failed to appreciate the humour, though. A voice came from a dark corner – in perfect English – 'Please comrade, no offence is meant.'

I turned to face a Polish colonel who continued: 'We all appreciate your kindness to us, and please accept our thanks and gratitude, but you see you gave a male urinal to a *Druga Itza* – a female comrade!'

I joined in the laughter and asked the colonel to tender my apologies. But how was one to know? The woman was in the uniform of a Partisan – battledress, trousers and close-cropped hair!

To help solve this problem, we acquired some empty potato tins. They were large and circular, similar to our large biscuit tins but with nice smooth rims, much to the delight of the patients.

Now, I leave it to you to appreciate the many difficulties we encountered. First and foremost was the language issue. Very few of the patients could understand our Italian, in which we were not at all proficient ourselves. Secondly, someone 'up top' had thought to provide a Serbo-Croat dictionary, which was of course useless under the present circumstances. Anyhow, we managed to get by with signs and gestures. Two Cockneys from the cookhouse tried their best to communicate, pointing to the food and yelling, 'GRUB!!' I will however, refrain from any further interpretations of these two well-meaning chaps, who became somewhat crude, even to us . . .

'Never let the side down, chaps!'

The last plane to arrive landed at dawn, just before 0500 hrs. Between then and 0800 hrs our time was fully taken up with re-dressing wounds and segregating the various cases to be conveyed by the large fleet of motor ambulances to the appropriate base hospitals.

One or two mutilated cases that needed plastic surgery were consigned to, of all places, East Grinstead in Sussex.

> *This is not the surprise it seems to have been, as Sir Archibald McIndoe (who had been honing the work started by his cousin Sir Harold Gillies during the Great War) was working at this hospital and was already well known for his treatment of the 'Guinea Pigs' – burned RAF aircrew who were treated at the Queen Victoria Hospital in East Grinstead.*

It was not until all the ambulances had left that we could have breakfast, strip, dropping our shorts and shirts into a bucket of petrol, wash in cold water and then crawl into bed to sleep and forget the night's tragedies.

I shall never forget one occasion, though, when a typical Sergeant exceeded his authority. Five of us had spent all night at the airfield reception, and just after the last of the patients had been dispatched and we were looking forward to collapsing onto our beds, this disciplinarian quashed our exhausted spirits, and ordered, to boost his ego, 'Before you lot get into bed, you can go round the airfield and pick up all the bits of paper that have been dropped by the evacuees.'

> *Sadly, it was, has been and will be, since Methuselah was a boy soldier, the lot of other ranks to fall foul of the Senior Non Commissioned Officers. Sergeants will 'beast' them, with scant regard to the needs of the service; it's because . . . on a number of occasions . . . they just can. They have an adage, 'The devil finds work for idle soldiers . . . and airmen!' All very well when they are sitting around in camp, but . . . Medical staff are seen by some as enjoying an 'easy life.' I can tell you from experience that, more often than not, it's the soldiers and airmen that get the easy bit!*

We were one of the many Allied units in Italy engaged in this 'mission of mercy.'

> *It is interesting to note this throwaway phrase in Rupert Clarke's book* With Alex at War: *'In spite of the supposed vows of chastity, the hospital was assisting many Yugoslav women soldiers having babies. This shows the varied cases we had flying in.'*

As the fighting subsided in the Balkans, flights were able to continue in daylight, which is when many of the pictures I have of this operation were taken.

> *Newspaper reports of the time gave the total number evacuated from Yugoslavia as over 10,000, but this was just the number of Tito's partisan casualties as of May 1944. Altogether some 50,000 individuals were evacuated by the Balkan Air Force Air Evacuation Service.*
>
> *There were a number of typhus epidemics in Yugoslavia at the time, covering areas including Bos, Dubice, Gradiska, Bihac and Sanski Most, and at the concentration camps in Jesonovac and Nova Gradiska, where, in the most appalling conditions, thousands died.*

✚

Priority Babies

I shall never forget the arrival of some fifty young children, or should I say 'tiny tots'. They arrived during the night accompanied by just a few women, some of whom were dressed in ill-fitting uniforms with heavy army boots which appeared miles too big. Others were wearing traditional heavy skirts, embroidered blouses and thick woollen socks. A few also had thin shoes made of woven straw. Others had no footwear at all.

We opened the door of the Dakota, and were taken aback with complete surprise as we saw the children sprawled across the floor covered with a few blankets. Some were still asleep, but despite the noise not a single one cried. They were between three and five years old.

We then observed that some of the women were holding very young babies in their arms. We had never even considered such a consignment. Above all else, we had not even thought for a second to pack nappies amongst the bandages and dressings. Surprisingly, all went well, and we got them off the plane in around an hour. Whilst we were unloading them, a few of the chaps spread five layers of blankets over the earth floor of one of the larger square tents. Within a very short time they had completely settled, curled up like tiny kittens with their bottoms resting in each other's tummies. As we carefully shut the tent flaps, they began to softly sing their own lullaby to themselves.

It would have been quite unnatural, of course, not be emotionally affected by them.

'Hark at those poor little bastards; far from home and their parents', whispered a voice in the dark.

It was of course far too dark to see the many hands wiping away something from the corner of their eyes . . .

The next morning, we made sure that they had a good breakfast of porridge and warm milk, and each child, regardless of age, was also given a bar of our own NAAFI ration chocolate before they were taken away in a convoy of ambulances to a special centre.

That morning, as we went to bed, we really felt that we had really achieved something more than usual that night.

✚

73 (Spitfire) Squadron, Cannae, Italy

As more territories in Yugoslavia were gradually liberated, night operations became unnecessary, although medical assistance continued. This was being undertaken by units far into the wild interior. We, therefore, returned to our normal duties at the hospital.

> *Between 1 July 1944 and 9 May 1945 – the date of the last operational mission – 38,089 sorties were flown and 2,000 tons of supplies were dropped monthly to Yugoslav troops and civilians.*

One morning, as I looked across the deserted beach towards the incoming tide, with the flat tinted clouds on the horizon, there was a definite drop in temperature. I felt an atmosphere of uncertainty. It was then I realised that autumn, the prelude to winter, was fast approaching.

Many of our patients had been discharged. I had been involved with a number of interesting cases, and the companionship which had developed, combined with the enjoyable evening discussions we had, was now sadly missed.

It was generally expected that the hospital would eventually be disbanded, and as such the staff became apprehensive about the future and the consequent parting with what were now old friends.

73 (SPITFIRE) SQUADRON, CANNAE, ITALY

One morning, I was notified that I had been posted, and not to another hospital but to a fully operational Spitfire Squadron! Transport had been arranged for the following morning.

'You can give up your shoes . . . where you're going, it will be gumboots all the way!' the Sergeant informed me with a wry smile. 'None of the amenities you've enjoyed here. It is going to be ruddy tough, but you will soon get used to it!'

73 Squadron was located some fifty miles into the interior of Italy, the nearest town being Termoli on the Adriatic coast.

On the day of departure, clouds of misty rain came down. This completely failed to lift anyone's morale. However, complete with full kit, plus a very heavy kitbag – and very thankful to be wearing my greatcoat – I clambered aboard the Jeep, next to the driver, and at 0800 hrs we set off to find my new quarters.

The journey was really rough, with rain and wind, added to which we had to negotiate precipitous Italian roads snaking their way through the countryside. We eventually reached the perimeter of the airfield, where we found a rough cinder track, just wide enough for one vehicle, with a vast amount of mud on either side of it. It reminded me of Salisbury Plain in the depths of winter.

(*This was the Field of Cannae, the site of the victory of Hannibal over the two Roman Consuls Varro and Paullus in 216 BC, where 80,000 died, following the first successful application of a novel manoeuvre – what is known today as a 'double envelopment', or 'pincer movement'.*) Looking back, I think that I nearly suffered a similar fate . . . if only psychologically!

We stopped to look for the familiar outlines of RAF buildings and tents, but were disappointed. All we could see was a caravan, beside which stood two tin shacks, and some distance away we could just discern a group of large ridge tents and a marquee surrounded by thick oozing mud.

'Is this the place?' enquired the driver.

By sheer luck we had observed a figure coming towards us – an airman, or 'Erk'. No civilian would have realised he was one of the station personnel, though. In fact, I would have defied anyone to recognise him as such! The only part of his attire which could in any way be described as 'uniform' was his dirty blue trousers, which were besmirched with dried mud He wore a sleeveless leather jerkin (*this was in fact standard RAF and indeed Army cold weather issue*), a woolly hat and scarf, together with a pair of gumboots which were half sunk into the mud.

'Where's sick bay?' I shouted.

He came closer and replied, pointing behind him with his thumb, 'That's sick bay.'

The driver and I looked at each other and both uttered the same expletive of surprise.

73 (SPITFIRE) SQUADRON, CANNAE, ITALY

Although I was hindered by my greatcoat, I managed to shoulder my kitbag and shouted a fond farewell to the driver. I then started to make my way towards the caravan with a despondent sigh. With much slipping and sliding, I finally reached one of the shacks and shouted:

'Anyone at home?'

The door was flung open, and there stood a Medical Orderly Corporal with a smile of welcome.

'Glad you've made it. Come on in!'

He stepped forward to relieve me of my burden and ushered me in to my new quarters. I was amazed to enter a nice cosy room, fully furnished and delightfully warm. The interior was lined with hardboard panels, to which were fixed cupboards and a drop-down table. At the far end was a two-tier wooden bunk. Apart from these essentials there was a doormat, a radio set and two electric light bulbs suspended from the rafters. Against the outer wall stood an empty ten-gallon oil drum, under which a petrol fire had been installed. On a small trestle table there rested an emergency petrol tank from a pranged kite (*downed and damaged aeroplane*). A feed pipe led to a fairly deep cake tin full of sand, into which flowed the spirit, drop by drop. The whole contraption resembled an oven, but because of the serious danger it posed, I think it inadvisable to give any further details! On one occasion I just managed to escape from an overflow of ignited petrol . . . minus my eyebrows and hair.

On the other side of the caravan was a similar building, again suitably furnished but with a camp bed rather than bunks. This was occupied by the Medical Officer, a tall young fellow of about twenty-five or twenty-seven. He was a jocular type with an infectious laugh. His diagnostic perception, I was to find, was excellent, considering he had recently qualified, and here he had been thrown into the deep end to deal with the burns and multiple injuries suffered by pilots. Serious cases, though, after stabilisation were rushed by field ambulance to the nearest base hospital, which more often than not was many miles away. In addition to emergency care, he was also responsible for the health and general cleanliness of the squadron. Then there was the customary sick parade at 0800 hrs each day to deal with.

Now to the so called 'caravan', which was in fact a converted large lorry chassis with a bespoke room on the back, much like the one Montgomery used as his 'Headquarters', seen in all the newsreels.

'Doc' McGrath, MO at 73 Sqn.

It had aluminium cupboards fitted on each side, with rows of ointments and medicines above. At the end backing onto the driver's compartment was a small office, with a typewriter and medical records storage. At the other end, by the door, hung a fire extinguisher.

73 (SPITFIRE) SQUADRON, CANNAE, ITALY

Above, below and overleaf: *The medical caravan and shacks at 73 Squadron.*

During the few months that I was with the Squadron in Italy, I witnessed tragedy and pathos. It was not all 'beer and skittles' by a long chalk. Other sections became involved: the Meteorological Officers, Flying Control Centre, the fire tender and of course the ambulance.

The important services rendered by the maintenance crews must not be forgotten either.

The only duty I did not relish was the 'Stand By' night operations duty. The ambulance and fire tender were at the take-off point of the runway. At dusk, it was our duty to be on the alert and watch each aeroplane take off and return. It became the custom as each one taxied past us for us to receive a wave of the hand, as well as sometimes a swish of the tailplane which would envelop us in a cloud of dust as spring and summer dried up the mud.

Each Spitfire carried a large capital letter on each side for identification. It was customary for each pilot to fly the same 'kite' – hence we would greet returning aeroplanes with, 'Here comes H for Harry; that will be Johnny!'

We waited for the last departure and then made ourselves comfortable. It was then a question of waiting, perhaps until dawn, for their return.

> *In late February 1944, before Scra was posted to 73 Sqn, a Wellington bomber got into trouble and had to make a forced landing at Cannae. The Wellington was carrying a full bomb load, and it crashed and caught fire immediately upon landing.*
>
> *LAC Jim McCabe, a Nursing Orderly like Scra and a friend of his, and Len Williams of the RAF Police were nearby and raced to assist the crew. In spite of the danger of exploding ammunition, they started to extract the crew. The rear gunner was brought out first, then the first of the bomb load exploded. McCabe was aware that others would go off soon, so went back into the burning aircraft and located another member of the crew, taking him out. When he was just yards away from the wreck, a second bomb exploded, destroying the remains of the plane. Jim and Len were awarded the George Medal for outstanding bravery in the face of danger. There were also two others who assisted that night.*

It was seldom that lights or flares were used on the runway, since there was always the risk of an enemy raider in the offing. So it was a nerve-wracking job keeping watch and listening for the return.

We sat in the driver's cabin of the ambulance on hard leather seats, with no heating and just an occasional mug of tea made on a small Primus stove. It was obvious that we would become drowsy, sitting out

Above and below: *Spitfires of 73 Squadron RAF/BAF.*

there for possibly the entire night, and so action was taken. We would take it in turns to prop ourselves in the corner of the cab for short periods of 'shut-eye'. Of course this was unknown to the 'powers that be'. Our engine was switched on and off at regular intervals throughout the night to ensure that there were no delays with a cold start.

After keeping vigil for several hours with the side windows open so that we could hear anything, we would become aware of the sound of an approaching plane. The sound of the Merlin engine is quite distinctive,

73 (SPITFIRE) SQUADRON, CANNAE, ITALY

Above and right: *In the first photo we can see Jim McCabe with Bob Peaty the driver and Scra, and in the next, Scra and Bob Peaty again in the thick mud.*

but this was a tense moment. We sat searching the sky for the first to return, and then someone would exclaim 'There she is!!' and point to the two pinpoint lights on the wing tips, shining dimly in the distance as the plane began to circle the airfield.

We would shout to the fire tender, 'Did you see her, Charley?'

An affirming 'Yes' was returned, and the engine of Charley's tender started revving in anticipation, in case there was a bad landing and a rescue was required.

It was just a question of watching those pinpoint lights on the wings – to see the pilot glide silently down, engine switched off, and then, if he's lucky, touch down, perhaps a few bumps then a taxi down the runway. We would all sigh with relief when an aircraft landed safely.

On one occasion a plane appeared to be coming in at the wrong angle, and we prepared to follow the tender in case there was an accident upon landing. However, the pilot corrected his approach and managed to touch down safely. We all heaved a collective sigh of relief. But the tension was still on and palpable. We had spotted another kite behind, which came in low but just managed to bank and miss the first arrival by a whisker.

Another time, a returning aircraft bounced on the runway whilst attempting a landing. The bounce upwards flipped the plane on to its back and it smacked down upon the runway. We went after him like greased lightning, but fortunately, the young pilot had managed to extricate himself in time. As he staggered away from the kite, there was a tremendous whoosh and explosion as the Spitfire turned into a huge ball of fire illuminating the night sky. Luckily, his injuries were superficial, and we raced him to sick bay. The most serious injury he suffered was psychological shock, for which special treatment was necessary. We were able to deal with this as we had a smaller tent nearby with a bed and fully equipped to deal with such a case. The young pilot officer was off flying duty for some ten days whilst he recuperated.

Of course, there were others whom, with the help of the fire crew, we were able to rescue from burning aircraft; and other pilots were found suffering from gunshot wounds but were lucky enough to survive and return to base after treatment at the main hospital. 'Drome Duty' was not a job we looked forward to. A hectic night could leave you exhausted and glad the night was over – to enjoy breakfast, followed by crawling into your bed and then, sleep.

The average age of these pilots was just twenty-three.

Strangely enough, we were never told of their targets. Sometimes they were on escort duty for a bombing raid; another time it was perhaps a reconnaissance to ascertain the strategic features of a potential target by photography. For example, the squadron were tasked with taking photographs before, during and after the attacks on Monte Cassino, the bombing of the town and the separate bombing of the famous 1,400-year-old Benedictine monastery. Some of the pictures taken by the squadron are shown here.

73 (SPITFIRE) SQUADRON, CANNAE, ITALY

Above and overleaf pages: *Before, during and after. 73 Sqn pictures of Monte Cassino.*

73 (SPITFIRE) SQUADRON, CANNAE, ITALY

Very soon after the capture of the monastery and town, the Doc and I were sent to help with the casualty clearance of the area, and I was able to see the devastation for myself. It was complete, and shocking and awe-inspiring at the same time. A once holy and ancient building had been reduced to piles of rubble. Thankfully, we did not stay long in this strange landscape of death and destruction, as our services were deemed surplus to requirements.

> *The necessity of bombing the town and monastery was discussed at length by the powers that be. It was to be a difficult and emotive question.*
>
> *The monastery formed part of the German 'Gustav' and 'Winter Line' – a heavily defended and fortified line which stretched across the Apennine Mountains, 100 miles south of Rome. This range formed a natural barrier, snaking its way almost from one side of the country to the other from east to west, and thus barred the Allies' advance towards Rome. At the centre of this line stood the imposing and strategically placed monastery. It covered all the main approaches, and an observer there could detect any slight movement in the Allied lines below for many miles around.*
>
> *There were actually four battles for the area in and around the monastery between January and May 1944, which saw some of the most bitter and intense fighting of the war. In fact, it is alleged that one German veteran of Stalingrad who was also at Cassino said the fighting there was much worse.*
>
> *The mountainous terrain prevented the execution of an original plan that would have encircled the monastery, with an attack coming from the north. The lack of the required mule transport was the deciding factor, as most of the area was impassable to road or even tracked vehicles. This meant that re-supply of troops in the forward areas would be virtually impossible, as it took a fully laden man almost five hours to bring up water, supplies and ammunition.*

73 (SPITFIRE) SQUADRON, CANNAE, ITALY

The Germans insisted that they were not in the monastery, but they did occupy the caves and areas of ground up to within 50 feet of the massive walls, which were 150 feet (46m) high and 10 feet (3m) thick. This fortress in all but name then stood atop a 1,700ft- high hill.

The decision to bomb the town and monastery was finally confirmed, and on 15 February 1944 the monastery was obliterated.

Sadly, the German paratroopers, the famous 'Fallschirmjäger' of the Luftwaffe, simply came out of their caves and shelters, reinforced their positions with the rubble, and held the ruins-cum-fortress for another three months.

You may ask what sort of recreation was available to these lads in such a bleak and lonely place. Well, we certainly had a marquee with a duckboard floor, electric light, and most importantly, a good-sized bar to lean on. Beer was in short supply, but this did not worry the chaps – they got a better kick out of two or three pints of a local brew of Vermouth. You may remember me touching upon this potent brew earlier on.

I would describe myself as a very moderate drinker, but I would agree with other members of the Squadron that we never tasted anything better. I am afraid to admit that my quota was but half a pint.

The CO's strict rule was no more than three pints, and no one was allowed to partake of a fourth, meaning that punishment for disobedience was severe. It would result in a court martial. The guilty party was unable to hide his sin, since without fail anyone drinking a fourth pint would pass out immediately! They would then remain unconscious for several hours, thus being no use to the Squadron or the war effort. I only had to deal with two such cases whilst serving with this Squadron.

Now, what about amusements? Well, there was darts, cards, shove ha'penny, dominoes, etc., plus bingo on a Saturday night.

The best and most popular attraction there, you would never guess... it was Ludo! There was a board, six feet square, with a design you would recognise, of squares and circles of varying colours. Two giant dice were used, which were shaken in a very large empty potato tin. Each colour represented a syndicate of four chaps. The stakes were high, and the shouts of excitement deafening. Everyone was very happy. I often felt that the motto of these young pilots was, 'Let us be merry, for tomorrow we may die.'

This sort of recreation did not suit everybody. Some would engage in a pastime or hobby such as wood carving, etc. One man resorted to knitting, despite the fun poked at him. He excelled at making decorative table mats (*most likely crocheted*) plus the ever popular 'bonce warmer' (*a bobble hat without the bobble*). He certainly had plenty of customers through the cold and wet winter!

Above and opposite: *Snow and mud at Cannae.*

73 (SPITFIRE) SQUADRON, CANNAE, ITALY

Winter 1944/1945, 73 Squadron

After a month of heavy rain, winter had really set in. Temperatures dropped well below freezing, followed by snow which formed drifts covering the wide deep ruts of rapidly freezing water and liquid mud.

The Doc and I did not wish to venture out of the hut at night in such deplorable conditions. We were snug and warm, the warmth and light provided by a small 'Aladdin' oil stove, while standing on the table was an oil-filled 'Tilley Lamp'.

Doc would sit relaxed with elbows on the table absorbed in a book. I sat opposite, endeavouring to put the finishing touches to several miniature watercolours before sending them home (*there is a profusion of these watercolours, which Scra painted onto small 6-inch by 4-inch postcard-sized 'canvases' – actually card. Many of them can be found reproduced throughout this book*), whilst appreciating the luxury of sipping hot sweet tea laced with a good tot of navy rum.

During the afternoon the Commanding Officer and Doc had visited each airman's tent and distributed a ration of rum, satisfying themselves that everyone was well protected and comfortable before nightfall.

Apart for the sound of rain or snow upon the roof of our tin hut, the camp appeared fairly quiet. There was just the occasional burst of laughter coming from a collection of ridge tents nearby, and the uproar of shouting from the canteen where an exciting game of Ludo was in progress.

As on every evening, our radio had been tuned to the BBC for the customary 'Nine o clock news' relayed from London which was our only real link with home. The ponderous strokes of 'Big Ben' resounded loudly throughout the camp, and yet, on this particular night, our 'old friend' sounded muffled.

'This is London calling!'

Doc in the medical tent.

Behind the voice we could discern the distant whine of air raid sirens. The Doc and I glanced at each other – 'Poor ******* devils', we both said, almost in unison.

It should be fairly easy for you to imagine our tense anxiety, being all those miles away from our loved ones, some of whom were of course in the capital itself. The whole camp fell silent. The news itself was good: our troops were advancing up the centre of Italy, and it was evident that Rome would be bypassed.

Due to the efforts of the US commander of the Fifth Army, Rome was NOT bypassed, as General Mark Clark had decided that it was too good a PR opportunity to miss. Rome was always a secondary objective for the Fifth Army, and the plan devised by Lieutenant General Harding was that the army would push north and east from the Anzio bridgehead, blocking the Germans' escape, thus trapping and destroying Kesselring's Tenth Army in a pincer movement. The capture of Rome was not the main thrust of the operation, but the cutting off of the German army was. As Churchill put it at the time in a telegram to Field Marshal Alexander, 'It's the cop (captured and killed number) that counts.'

This, though, was not the foremost thought in General Clark's mind. He appeared dismissive of the fate of this German army, and with the Allied troops within four miles of cutting off the German withdrawal and boxing them in on all sides, he thought it better to divert himself and one of his Army Corps to Rome. Thus the official plan of the operation was not executed, and the Germans couldn't believe their luck. Clark alone had coveted the achievement of capturing the first Axis capital to fall to Allied forces. It would be him, not the massed forces of the Allies, not the British, whom he despised and mistrusted, not the Poles who had captured Monte Cassino, nor the French, Canadian, New Zealanders or South Africans, nor yet the Indians, who had all contributed heavily – and at great cost– in opening up Italy. Interestingly, the British Army contributed as many divisions to the Fifth Army as there were US Divisions; only one third of the Fifth Army consisted of US troops.

In a massive 'hissy fit' Clark warned his commander, Field Marshal Alexander, that if he had to share the headlines with any of the Allies he would refuse his orders, and if any members of the British (made up of Commonwealth, Empire and French troops) Eighth Army were to advance towards Rome before him, he was ready, and very willing to issue orders to his (US) men in the Fifth Army to open fire on non-American troops!

Whilst advancing towards Rome he ensured he was incommunicado, even to the extent of leaving his wireless and wired communications equipment 'off the hook' so that he could not be contacted, and hiding his intent for 24 hrs from his commanding officer, Alexander.

This was patently mutinous, but Alexander ignored this outburst, all for the greater Allied good.

Clark entered Rome on 5 June, unopposed. Rome had been declared an 'Open City' by the Germans, meaning that it would not be fought over, and thus the destruction of the ancient city as well as the Holy See was avoided.

He had earlier in the battle for Italy felt robbed of a 'glorious entry' into Naples as its sole liberator, so he made sure that this 'liberation party' was all about him. He had a Public Relations entourage of some fifty members, as well as a personal photographer whom he kept by his side at all times. This photographer was only allowed to take shots from the General's left, which Clark considered his best side. The pictures of Mark Clark climbing the steps of the Capitol in Rome, which made him famous, were not taken by any of his entourage, though; they were taken by a young British Army officer of the Army Film and Photographic Unit, one Alan Whicker, who went on to present the acclaimed and popular television series 'Whicker's World', and later, in the twilight of his career, a no-holds-barred, poignant, pithy – but with an understated wit – programme about his Army career, 'Whicker's War'.

Clark's decision to enter Rome has been widely regarded as one of the worst military blunders of the war, and one taken just to satisfy an ego. More than 140,000 Germans were broken and in full retreat. His egotistical decision ensured that the Germans could regroup, rearm and fight on for another year – another year of unnecessary deaths, woundings and destruction throughout Italy, which included large numbers of civilians, as well as those of German and Allied troops.

One can quite easily imagine, given the almost Dunkirk-style escape of the Germans, that somewhere in a drawer in the Reichstag sat a box, with Mark Clark's name on it – containing an Iron Cross . . .

A Winter's Tale

'I shouldn't be surprised to see more snow by morning', I said.

The Doc looked up from his book with a frown of displeasure.

'Don't you think we have enough problems, Harry? We already have plenty on our hands; we've two men down with the 'flu, and Tom the mechanic from the MT (*Motor Transport*) with the abdominal pains which could well be appendicitis. I went down to them an hour ago, and I am not happy with their conditions at all.'

He continued, 'I think you had better contact Bob, and tell him to get the ambulance ready. We'll take them into the Base Hospital.' (*'Bob' has been Identified as Bob Peatey, and is seen in the photograph on page 115*).

'What???!!' I exclaimed 'Tonight?? In this weather?? We could easily get bogged down in mud or a snow drift.'

I felt somewhat apprehensive at this plan, to put it mildly.

'We will have to chance that, I'm afraid', said Doc.

'Take a Thermos flask of tea, with plenty of sugar in case they get cold, and perhaps a tot of rum may come in handy; It could take a couple of hours to do the round trip . . . if we are lucky. Oh, and tell Bob to chuck in a couple of shovels, just in case we need them.'

'Thanks VERY much', I replied, a little crestfallen at the prospect of such a journey, in this weather.

The Doc grinned widely at me.

'Don't worry, I'm coming too!'

Bob backed the ambulance as near as he could to the two tents where the patients lay, picking his way through the existing ruts in the mud towards the entrances. We then carried the three men on stretchers into the 'Blood Tub', as the ambulances were known. I must admit Bob managed it very well – and did a damned good job of bringing the tub as close as he did.

Doc sat up front with Bob the driver, and I made myself as comfortable as I could in the back with the three patients.

It was quite a journey, somewhat slow and ponderous due to the weather, and on occasion I was forced to throw myself across the patients to keep them prone as we bumped up and down the varying peaks and troughs of the deep ruts in the thick, oozing mud.

After a somewhat nerve-wracking journey, we made it to the main road, and ultimately reached the 50th British General Hospital at Termoli. After disposing of our patients at reception, we were kindly offered bowls of hot soup and freshly baked bread by Matron; but bearing in mind the prevailing conditions, we politely refused, although we appreciated and took up the offer of having our Thermos replenished. Naturally, we were very anxious to get back to camp and relax into the comfort of our own warm hut.

This was only one of several trips that we made to 50th BGH, including a number with young pilots, wounded and suffering from severe burns. Luckily, the majority of these trips were made during the warmth of an Italian summer's day, when the roads and tracks were passable, and the light breeze bought some small comfort to those in the rear of the 'Tub'.

Generally speaking, the health of the airmen during the winter was remarkably good. Naturally, there were those who reported sick with no more than a cough and cold. While chatting with the doc, the subject of the general health of the squadron was paramount, with consideration to the climate and living conditions.

But . . . neither of us had considered the possibility of being taken ill ourselves, until one day the Doc developed a 'shorter' (*shortness of breath*). As usual, no antibiotics or other precautions had been taken.

> *Penicillin was then seen as the new wonder panacea for all ills. It was prescribed as a prophylaxis i.e. 'just in case'. Sadly, this built up over the decades an antibiotic resistance, which we are seeing today in some sepsis cases and other problems, and is causing horrendous problems in both hospitals and patients. In this case, though, a prescription of antibiotics would have definitely been indicated.*

As most service personnel would say, and Doc was no different, he repeated the same mantra they all do: 'Oh, I'll be all right.' But I insisted upon him taking the maximum dose (*what we would call a loading dose today*) of M&B tablets.

> *This was a pre-penicillin antibiotic. M&B 693 was developed in Britain and first prescribed in 1938 to treat pneumonia. It was manufactured by May and Baker of Dagenham, hence M&B. The most famous patient in these initial days was the Prime Minister, Winston Churchill himself, who contracted pneumonia during the war. The drug most likely saved his life, and its success was widely reported in the press.*

After a lengthy argument, I managed to get him bedded down, and treated him just like any other patient of mine, as I was accustomed to in hospital.

His temperature began to climb, and he had every sign and symptom of bronchitis. I did not sleep in my bunk but managed to get some rest sitting in his canvas chair with a blanket. I was taking observations every four hours (*'4 hourly obs'*), which included taking his temperature, pulse, respirations and blood pressure, and recording them on a chart.

He now realized that his condition had deteriorated and asked for hot kaolin poultices to be applied to relieve the congestion.

> *I feel I must say a word or two here about poultices, as they are not very well known these days. They had been used since time immemorial to treat all sorts of ailment, from an abscess to dog bites and all points between, including all types of wounds and infections.*
>
> *A poultice is a moist concoction which is usually heated and spread upon an injury, ache, or wound and held in place with a cloth. It used to be known also as a 'plaster', when the poultice was smeared on a bandage before application. This is the 'paper plaster' that Jack had applied after tumbling down the hill with Jill.*
>
> *In this case, the infected pleurae giving rise to pleuritic pain may be given relief by the application of a poultice, held in place by a 'many-tailed bandage'. The pleurae are the linings in the chest that surround each lung and separate*

them from the thoracic wall. They form two layers of thin serous membranes. A many-tailed bandage is basically what it says . . . a bandage with a central large area and a number of rolls coming off it, instead of the usual one each side of the dressing. These are then tied off or fixed with tape to hold the central large area in place on the body of the patient.

The application of the poultices was continued throughout the night. Early the next morning, his temperature began to go down, but I was still very concerned and suggested that he be taken to the hospital in Termoli. This he stoutly refused with many descriptive adjectives. (*It is always said that doctors and nurses make the worst, most objectionable and argumentative patients!*).

It took nearly ten days to get him fit and on his feet again – as it had turned into pneumonia – but as each day passed, progress was maintained.

During the period of his illness I took over the customary morning sick parade, with the help of the air crew. Luckily, the weather for flying was putrid, which made my task much easier. These chaps kept the caravan and huts clean and helped to organise the meals, etc. for us. I felt sure that they enjoyed the experience of being a medical or nursing orderly, and the chance to escape a far worse complaint . . . boredom. I also noticed that those reporting sick diminished each day. I wonder if my assistants may have been a little over-zealous on those reporting?

During one period of extreme cold, with frozen mud and snow, the squadron received a signal from air headquarters enquiring why a particular wing had failed to support a certain bombing attack. The answer given, supported by medical grounds, was that the squadron had become grounded due to lack of fuel. The fuel had been used to provide warmth to the personnel of the squadron during severe winter conditions under canvas, since it was feared that casualties and deaths by freezing were otherwise inevitable.

Interlude: Ablution Supreme

The Corporal who had greeted me upon arrival with 73 Squadron at Cannae had been with them throughout the North Africa campaign from Egypt to El Alamein, and thence to Italy. Never before had I met such a versatile character; he could master any task set before him, and we could depend upon his skill in any circumstances. His accent and voice betrayed his birth. He was a 'Taffy' born and bred in a small village in Wales, and this name was the one he had gone by since joining up . . . as would so many before and after him.

> *The name 'Taffy' can be traced back to and early Nursery Rhyme which begins thus:*
> *Taffy was a Welshman,*
> *Taffy was a thief,*
> *Taffy came to our house*
> *And stole a side of beef!*
>
> *The name is thought to have come from the River Taff that rises in the Brecon Beacons, before flowing into the Severn Estuary at Cardiff.*

It was he who had built the two tin shacks which served as the medical centre, in a manner and with a luxury which one would have expected to find in a small cottage back home.

It was the custom of the medical services of the forces (*and still is!*) to maintain personal cleanliness at all times, in all theatres of war, in spite of the varying climatic conditions. Of course, in the heart of the desert this was difficult given the shortage of water. So, whilst in North

Africa, the ritual was to stand in a galvanised bowl which only contained enough water to cover the feet.

The simple procedure was to place the bowl of water in the fierce rays of the sun for only a few minutes, whilst taking care not to over-expose it, or the water would take too long to cool. Even in the shade the temperature would rise to 100 degrees Fahrenheit, and even a cup of water would become warm very quickly.

Standing naked in the bowl for a 'sponge-down' was the nearest we came to a sumptuous bath at this time.

In the winter at Cannae, it was quite a different matter. We were then exposed to bitterly cold winds, with snow and liquid mud all around us. One day, Taffy came up with a brilliant idea. (*This of course is NOT to be tried at home in your back garden!*)

He acquired an empty 50-gallon petrol drum. He proceeded to cut it in half, and upon one half he attached two handles of thick, plaited wire. Now of course the question arose, how were we to obtain the necessary quantity of hot water? The next step was to dig a hole a couple of yards away from the hut; the improvised bath was then placed over the hole and supported by several large stones. A sufficient quantity of ice-cold water was poured in . . . then came the final touch, and a highly dangerous one!

A half pint of aviation fuel was poured into the hole under this makeshift bath, and the order was given by Taffy: 'Stand clear, everybody!'

He then tossed a lighted match underneath the contraption, and following the resulting explosion the water reached boiling point. Whilst this was in operation, Taffy, Bob Peaty, the ambulance driver, I and three other chums queued up. We had previously made room in our small hut for the bath, and it was gingerly carried in via the two-wire-handled contraption.

Sadly, I only knew Taffy for a short time, as he was 'posted out' soon after this incident (transferred to another unit). He was sadly missed.

I think that this posting was the happiest of all, in spite of the rough conditions.

The Squadron Farewell and on to Yugoslavia

Conditions were generally rather grim during the winter months. Towards the end of February, the weather improved and we observed that the sunny periods became more frequent and the air temperature began to climb. The Allies were making progress, advancing rapidly northwards through Italy. It was a foregone conclusion that the Squadron would cease to operate from Cannae.

Within a few weeks of this, a section of the Squadron was also posted for a time to Piraeus in Greece, and thence on to Malta.

Then the day came when the news spread throughout the camp that we were on the move. Little did we know of our destination, until the following day.

The chill of an early spring morning and the golden shafts of sunlight bought cheer and expectancy to those packing the equipment and making sure that their own kit and personal belongings were on the waiting lorries. Those that had been loaded were gradually making their way to the cinder-track perimeter road, to form into a long convoy. No one would have thought this convoy was a military one. Each vehicle was packed high with all shapes and sizes of cases, parcels, boxes and, above all, sitting on the top, wooden slatted crates and cages of pets, including cats, dogs, chickens, ducks and birds – not forgetting the Squadron's parrot mascot, perched high, right on top of everything, screeching its ruddy head off!

Doc had earlier mentioned that morning that our small medical unit would not be joining the convoy. We were to proceed, well in front of the main convoy, and then take ship at the port of Bari with the ambulance plus a lorry, which was packed to capacity with tents and all the necessary equipment. We were then duly dispatched upon a secret assignment . . . to the interior of Yugoslavia to join a medical mission to the partisans.

> *This was Operation Bingham, in which Doc and Scra were part of 281 Wing RAF, and ostensibly part of 30 MFH. The signs for 281 Wing can be seen in Scra's pictures that follow.*

The journey to Bari took about three or four hours, and as soon as we reached the quayside we went straight on board a LCT (*Landing Craft, Tank*). We backed on so we could get off more easily at our point of destination. We were then joined by several 'GDs', Ground Staff for General Duties.

We sailed away, silently, all alone and upon calm water, with the gentle throb of the craft's engine. It was very difficult to estimate our speed, and it all seemed to be unusually quiet and peaceful . . . so much so that we were able to enjoy the antics of two dolphins weaving and diving at the prow the whole way. In addition, as we peered over the side, we gazed down through the clear water into the sunlit depths and were able to see very clearly flashes of silver as the sun caught fish deep down in the sea. It was a fascinating journey, and I think a most enjoyable one.

The LCT was now moving very slowly, weaving silently through the chain of small islands that are dotted along the Yugoslav coastline. We were then told to keep quiet, as some of the islands might still be occupied by the enemy and we ran the risk of being fired upon, particularly around the island of Pag. Slowly we crept along, getting nearer to our destination, but with anxiety about what could happen before we got there. Two Royal Navy seamen manned the pair of .50 calibre machine guns either side of the bridge at the rear of the craft. They moved around the gun mount cautiously yet earnestly, looking out for any threats from the enemy.

Thankfully, everything went according to plan, and we eventually reached our destination. As we began to pull into the white stone quay, a group of small red-roofed houses began to come into view. We had arrived at the village of Zara (Zarda).

THE SQUADRON FAREWELL AND ON TO YUGOSLAVIA

On the quayside, a group of partisans gave an enthusiastic wave of welcome and eagerly assisted with the unloading of the LCT. They were devoid of a 'uniform' as such; perhaps one could recognise a pair of patched khaki trousers or a dirty battledress jacket, and a few wore the traditional Yugoslav field service cap. The only 'uniformity' was the five-pointed red star badge pinned to their caps. This was our first contact with the brave citizen army of Tito in their own country.

Our first obstacle was that none of our crew spoke Serbo-Croat, so with some difficulty we explained ourselves in a form of Italian. Eventually, when some sort of understanding between us was reached, combined with many gestures, they directed us to their landing strip, several miles inland.

The surrounding countryside was rough and rugged, mostly covered in heather and gorse. There was one track through, and it led us to the improvised runway, which was just wide enough for one Spitfire. It was simply a flattened dirt track, surrounded by stakes of rough wood and rope.

'We simply can't camp here', commented Doc gloomily.

I turned and pointed to a range of hills not so far away, and upon the top of one, a small plateau, which appeared to me to be the ideal site for our operations. From there we could easily and safely observe the approach of any aircraft.

The last rays of the setting sun urged us on to erect our two large tents in which we intended to sleep. We found the roof section – but failed to find the necessary poles. We found wooden tent pegs galore and a wooden mallet, the wall sections, but no poles, so one roof section was strung up under the tree branches to give us some shelter for the night.

Yes, we managed a meal – of sorts – and a brew-up of tea, and then bedded down on the hard stony ground, listening to the soft, sweet lullaby of the nightingales above our heads. Cheerfully they sang all night, and hardly a wink of sleep was got by anyone. We tried to frighten them away, but they always came back to lull us to sleep with their song – which they didn't.

One bright chap suggested empty tins with stones inside, which could be suspended from the branches and might frighten them away. It didn't. They came and went throughout the night. The noise and clatter of the stones in cans, augmented by the fluttering and song of the birds, kept us well and truly awake until dawn. Please don't remind me who saw this area as an 'ideal' site.

At the first blush of morning, the birds had flown away and all was peace within and without. Well, no, not quite. As we began to fall asleep, one of our party whispered – for everyone to hear:

'Can you hear the sea?'

'Don't be so daft!' came a reply. 'We're miles away from any salt water!'

I was awake and I sat up, peering out from under our shelter. I looked and held my breath then crawled over to find Doc, woke him and pointed.

'Look at that mob!'

A great multitude of men, women, and children, including babes in arms, possibly numbering well over a couple of hundred, were sitting on a mound – waiting for medical treatment!

We couldn't blame them. Some ruddy fool had planted our big red cross flag nearby.

The first big problem: 'They must be hungry, what can we give them to eat?'

As Doc and I walked toward them, the whole multitude was silent. Doc reached for his small paperback dictionary.

'*Zdravo, Duge!*' ['Greetings, Comrade!']

One of the men followed up in a form of Italian and explained that news of our arrival had spread and had prompted the sick, lame, wounded and hungry to come for help.

First and foremost, it was feed the hungry and give them something to drink. Luckily we had a Soyer stove, full of hot tea. To our dismay, no one there had ever tasted tea before, and to our further dismay, none of the assembled crowd stepped forward to taste it, so the whole lot was thrown away.

> *Soyer Stoves had been a mainstay of the British Army since the Crimean war of 1854–56. They had been invented by the head chef of the Reform Club in London, Alexis Soyer. The military expedition to the Crimea had been a disaster (Charge of the Light Brigade, etc.): almost 16,500 of the deaths had been from disease; a further 2,700 were killed in action, and 2,000 had died of wounds. It was a national scandal. Florence Nightingale went out to improve the standard of medical care, and Soyer to improve and reorganize the victualling of the army. Soyer was the best known cook of his time, what we would call today a 'Celebrity Chef'. He wrote books, designed model kitchens, and more.*
>
> *At this time army rations were handed men individually, and they were expected to cook them over an open fire. This system hadn't much changed since early medieval times, and Soyer designed a novel stove to cook rations on as a group (actually one Soyer would feed almost two platoons of soldiers, or fifty men).*
>
> *The Soyer could boil twelve gallons of water in under ten minutes, which was a necessity at all times with British forces . . . for tea. It could also cook food on a hot plate, which could be placed on top of the boiling water, and*

twelve gallons of soup or stew could be cooked in the boiling pot, which resembled a large cauldron and slipped into the top of the stove. The stove itself resembled a large upended drum, with a door and grate at the bottom, and a large offset chimney protruding from one side at the top. Soyers would burn anything that came to hand: wood, rags, even dried camel dung!

Soyer was credited with saving more lives than Florence Nightingale in the Crimea, and his legacy lived on in the Army for over 120 years. His stoves were used in every theatre of war in which British, Empire and Commonwealth troops fought up until the Falklands campaign. Sadly, the main stock of Soyer stoves went down with the Atlantic Conveyor *in 1982. Some remained and they can be found around the country on occasion. They are used by a number of 'living historians', and I can vouch for their efficacy. I used to own one, and even cooked a huge fried breakfast for a number of friends on the top of mine, and once a gigantic paella!*

Not to be disheartened, we handed round our spare rations of biscuits and 'bully beef' and gave cold water to those who were thirsty.

At the same time, we selected those who most needed urgent medical attention, whom we could attend to that day. We then explained to their leader, in broken Italian, that those sick whom we had not selected as the most urgent cases could return the next day, and we would endeavour to obtain a supply of special medications such as the M&B tablets which I mentioned earlier.

A dispatch rider was sent back to the quayside with a handwritten message which was to be handed over to the captain of the next British boat to arrive. We requested a good supply of medications, but emphasised that the main priority was food. And lots of it.

The next morning, supplies were dropped by parachute by one of our aircraft, and quantities of food arrived by boat . . . in which coffee was the priority. A message also arrived stating that a medical team comprising two more doctors was on its way to assist us and would arrive the following day.

THE SQUADRON FAREWELL AND ON TO YUGOSLAVIA

THE SQUADRON FAREWELL AND ON TO YUGOSLAVIA

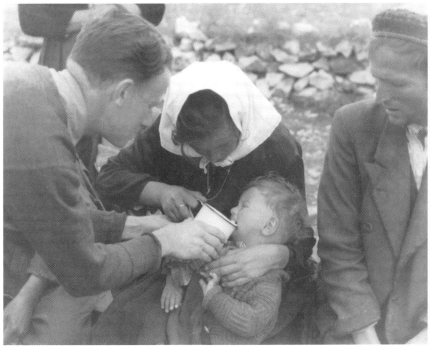

NURSING AT THE FRONTLINE

THE SQUADRON FAREWELL AND ON TO YUGOSLAVIA

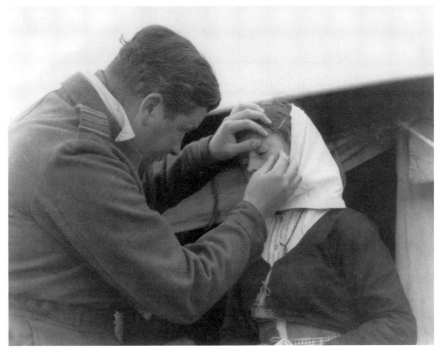

NURSING AT THE FRONTLINE

THE SQUADRON FAREWELL AND ON TO YUGOSLAVIA

Gradually, the number of those needing treatment decreased each day. We still had our emergencies to deal with, though.

Early one morning, a Mustang fighter plane landed on the airstrip. The young South African pilot had been badly shot up, and we had difficulty in releasing him from his seat. Fortunately, we had erected a large square tent close by for such an emergency which was fitted out with a single bed and medical supplies. We fought hard to pull him through – but were desperately sorry and very disappointed that we failed. I wrote a letter to his parents, and received a very sad reply (*below*).

THE SQUADRON FAREWELL AND ON TO YUGOSLAVIA

Now, whether it is Scra's memory that failed him at this point, or a deliberate attempt to conceal identities (as he had done many times before for confidentiality), I know not, but it took a long time to trace this pilot, and I had to resort to the good offices of a South African genealogical page on Facebook, of which I am a member. The marvellous offices of one of the members from South Africa are acknowledged at the beginning of this book.

Thankfully, the address is almost obvious, and the first name of the sender is completely so.

The pilot has been identified via the scant details on the letter, such as his first name, the first name of his mother, the name of the farmstead, the name of the town, and the fact he had a sister. He was Lieutenant Michael Duchen, of 43 Squadron South African Air Force, flying with the Balkan

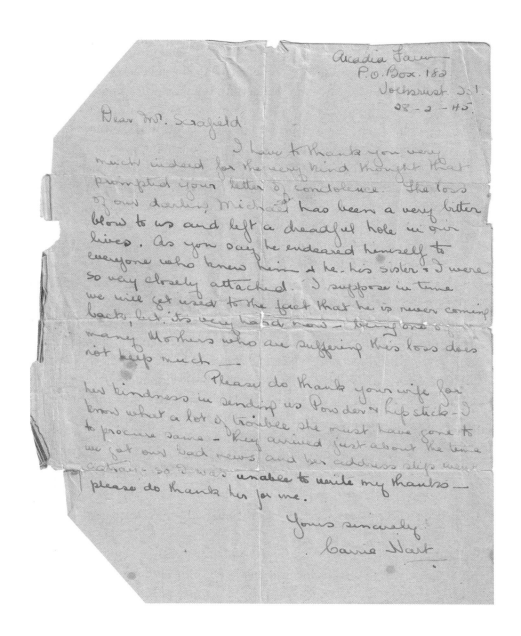

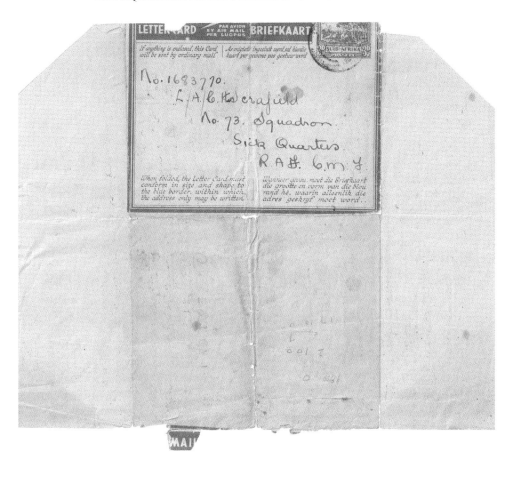

Air Force, which was part of the joint Allied force serving in the eastern Mediterranean area.

The problem is that all the available data and records which reference Lt Duchen state that his place of injury and subsequent death was not in Yugoslavia. The records of the South African War Graves Project, and indeed those of the CWGC, state he was in a Spitfire MkVIII (JF887), and that he 'died in an accident when his aeroplane crashed upon landing after dark, with illumination provided by truck lights . . . at Florence Peretola airfield' on 02 October 1944 . . . which is now the main airport for Florence.

Scra was nowhere near this airfield at this time, and the date is prior to his landing in Yugoslavia; indeed, the letter *shown above with its February 1945 date is also prior to his attachment. I have made an awful lot of enquiries, but I think that this may be something misremembered. A lot of aeroplanes of all sorts and sizes crash-landed at Cannae in various states of distress, as the reader may remember from the case of the Wellington and the awarding of two George Medals to members of 73 Squadron. If this is an amalgam of several forced landings we may never know, but Scra certainly cared for Lieutenant Duchen somewhere, as the letter attests.*

The war was drawing to a close, and enemy forces began a rapid withdrawal from the occupied territories, which of course included Yugoslavia.

Our essentials, including food and medical supplies, were now more plentiful, and the peasants and partisans who had depended upon the Allies for assistance began to return to their homes. Consequently, very few were now coming to us for medical treatment.

Late one afternoon, a signal came through from our headquarters in Italy:

'Drop everything, make for the coast, flash a torch and a Naval craft will pick you up. THIS IS URGENT!'

Naturally we were dumbfounded. These poor peasants had become our friends. We had helped to feed them and give medical assistance whenever possible. You will observe from my photographs the kind of people – which included young children and babes in arms – that came to us. Some arrived soon after daybreak, having walked through rough country for miles, most of them wearing the traditional footwear made from rushes.

Suddenly, though, with much surprise and without warning, we had received this signal, after only a month there. We found out later that the evacuation had been ordered due to a 'difference of opinion' between Marshal Tito and the Allies. It was decided that our small team would disperse and try to proceed to the nearest coastline without delay.

The sun was slowly sinking, sending its last golden rays low down behind the trees, from which one could hear the nightingales begin their nocturnal chorus. Yet, in spite of all this beauty, and the calm stillness of the approaching night, a few anxious humans were planning their escape from possible capture and execution.

Doc and I decided to take the ambulance down the narrow track and chance our luck by making our way across the rough moorland whenever possible. First and foremost, we tied a Red Cross flag to the side of the windscreen, hoping that this would give us some protection from any trigger-happy partisans we might come across. Doc took the driver's seat, armed with a Sten gun and plenty of spare ammo. It was agreed that I would travel in the back among the stretchers and blankets, armed to the teeth with two revolvers, two Lee Enfield rifles and a large amount of ammo for these weapons, which had different sized rounds to the Sten.

'Pick up those rifles, Harry, and that box of ammo and hop in the back. If we are stopped, I'll tell them I'm taking a dead comrade back for burial. Let's hope to God that they believe me.'

I jumped into the back, making sure that the double doors were securely fastened, and then stood with my back against the wooden partition behind the driver's seat. Sliding back the small observation panel, and standing facing the double door, I could keep in contact with the Doc.

In spite of the weapons, I must admit that the chances of survival were slim if we encountered a group of partisans with orders.

We were compelled to proceed slowly and carefully across the rough tundra-like landscape until we came to the narrow track. We were then able to increase our speed, cautiously, to avoid any suspicion from nearby locals.

'Here comes trouble', whispered the Doc.

A group were wandering aimlessly in our direction, and when we came into their view, they spread out across the track. We slowed down but had no intention of stopping. Their leader shouted at us in Italian to stop and be identified.

'Get ready, Harry . . . This certainly looks like trouble. Don't open the windows until I start firing, then you can blast like hell', Doc said in a very determined voice.

Doc greeted the leader in reply to their challenge but he did not stop.

He put on a disarming smile and shouted to him, '*Stravo, Druge*!' followed by '*Hospitalli*' in Italian, pointing down the narrow track.

Some of the partisans stepped aside, but a number held their ground in a line across the track, bringing us to a sudden halt.

I stood with my back firmly against the partition, a revolver in each hand, cocked and ready. Suddenly I heard footsteps pass by the side window, heading towards the rear doors. A hand descended upon the door handles . . . then, just as I readied myself for whatever was to happen, I heard the voice of their leader. What he said I don't know, but the doors remained closed, and Doc slowly released the brakes. The partisans stepped out of the way and waved us on. God had certainly answered my silent prayers that evening.

'Good on you, Doc!' I shouted as we continued on our nerve-wracking journey.

We had been travelling for about an hour after this, taking short cuts across country, when we returned to the road.

It was close on midnight when we eventually reached a deserted stretch of beach. The stillness of the night was unnerving. There was no moon, but the visibility was surprisingly good. However, there were no ships in sight. We sat close together and patiently waited, flashing our torch at intervals across the calm sea. An hour sped by, but there was still no sign of any naval craft whatsoever. We were beginning to become anxious, and continued to flash our torch at intervals, not wishing to exhaust the only battery we had.

Suddenly a searchlight swung round unexpectedly, striking us and illuminating us in its blinding light. We waved our arms about in jubilation now that the suspense was over. Within minutes, a Landing Craft, Tank (LCT) became visible to us on the shoreline, and slowly inched its way towards us. As it got nearer, we could see the boarding platform being lowered, and we drove onto it with ease, both of us exhaling almost in unison a deep sigh of relief.

The captain came forward to greet us and offered a most welcome large tot of navy rum, which we eagerly accepted. Within a matter of minutes we were sailing almost silently in the direction of Italy. In fact, the ship reached the port of Ancona in record time.

We slid silently alongside the quayside, deserted apart from one lonely figure who emerged from the shadows and walked slowly forward towards the gangplank. Much to our surprise, it was a very smartly dressed RAF officer, in a highly pressed khaki drill uniform; the creases in his trousers were sharp enough to cut bread with!

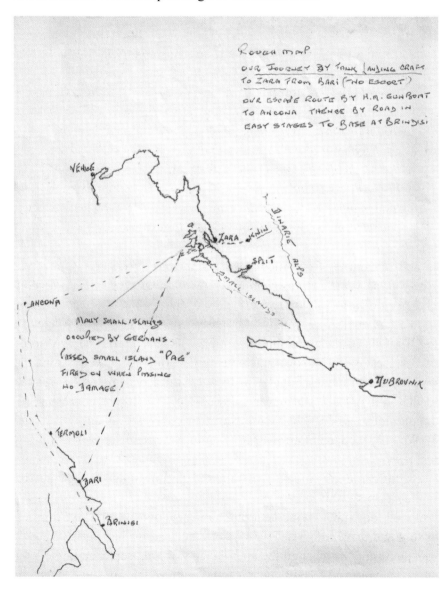

THE SQUADRON FAREWELL AND ON TO YUGOSLAVIA

He proceeded to give us instructions that we were to proceed south with our ambulance to the RAF Transit Camp at Brindisi, and report there for further instructions.

However, we both felt very deeply the after-effects of tension and anxiety that we had endured on the journey from our camp in Yugoslavia. Doc made a suggestion:

'To hell with his damnable instructions! We are going to make own way, in our own time.'

> *There is very little in the history books about the SOE Medical Mission to the Balkans. There is plenty in the works I have listed in the bibliography at the end of this book on the whys and wherefores of the Balkan campaign, the capture of British troops by Partisans at gunpoint, the argument over Trieste and the beginning of the Cold War, but there is only one book on the Medical Mission:* Guerilla Surgeon *by Lindsay Rogers. I heartily commend this book to the reader. Even then, there is little mention of the primary care unit set up by Scra and his chums from 73 Sqn/281 wing. A sadly forgotten episode.*

In fact, the journey from Ancona to Brindisi took us ten days. (*The direct route on the modern autostrada is some 360 miles, and would allegedly take five and a half hours today!*)

We passed through many extremely pretty and quaint villages in the foothills of the Apennine mountains, picking up on the way some of the local very intoxicating beverage, Vermouth, directly from the vineyards en route to Foggia. In fact, I think I became quite immune to the stuff myself, and never suffered the 'fourth pint court martial' unconsciousness that I had witnessed previously at Cannae!

We only stopped at army or RAF units for essentials such as rations and petrol.

Spring came early in southern Italy, and the mud gradually disappeared in the warm sunshine.

I well remember an incident that happened one evening. We decided to stop and drive into a dell away from the road we had been taking. It was dusk, and we ensured the ambulance was well screened in the long grass and amongst the silhouette of the tall trees that surrounded us.

We enjoyed our evening meal, such as it was, army rations washed down by our customary mug of hot sweet tea, after which it was time to bed down for the night. I climbed into the back of our trusty 'Blood Tub' and began to prepare our beds. Turning back towards the doors, I found to my amazement that a nearby field was alight, the colour of electric blue. I beckoned the Doc over.

'What's up Harry?' he asked.

I just looked across to the field and pointed.

'Well', he said, 'haven't you seen this before? It's fireflies.'

Having spent all of my life in and around London, it was not something I had seen. I had never camped out in the countryside, away from the bustle of an RAF station before. It was truly a wonderful sight. After a few minutes staring in awe, we crawled under our mosquito nets. Within seconds, the flies had covered the outer skin of the nets, bathing us in a brilliant blue light. It was actually bright enough to read a newspaper by, even at midnight.

We continued to bypass the major towns, through to Campobasso, some 50 miles inland from the airfield at Termoli.

THE SQUADRON FAREWELL AND ON TO YUGOSLAVIA

A view of General Alexander's Headquarters at Casserta.

We then took the familiar coastal route down to Bari, and finally reached the Transit Camp, which was situated amongst the many olive trees on the outskirts of Brindisi.

Here we parted company for at least a couple of weeks. Doc was accommodated in a small officer's tent on an adjoining site, and consequently I saw very little of him, even though we were both still on the nominal roll of 73 Squadron.

In Brindisi at the end of the journey.

Brindisi

I was fortunate to find myself billeted in a tent with a very interesting companion, and we soon became friends.

We went into the town of Brindisi quite often, visiting the principal shops, and the famous Opera House. Here we enjoyed all the popular operas and the ENSA shows that were specially provided for the troops.

ENSA (Entertainments National Service Association, or as it was known to the troops on active service, Every Night Something Awful) was an organization initially set up in 1939 to provide entertainment for the troops, and it came under the NAAFI umbrella (Navy Army and Air Force Institutes). Most of the great stars of the period performed at one time or another, sometimes from the backs of trucks and lorries very close to the front – so close, in fact, that that they had to wear military uniform in case they were captured by the enemy and assumed to be spies! Acts included the big bands of Geraldo and Mantovani and the top singers such as Jessie Matthews, George Formby, Vera Lynn and even Noel Coward. Theatrical entertainments were put on with Hollywood stars such as Laurence Olivier too.

Some entertainments were not of the standard reached by the above, and small trios of well-meaning old ladies could sometimes be found playing slightly off key, but doing their best for the troops – not always to the greatest reception!

As always, there was a snag . . . how to return to camp after an evening out!

The camp itself was situated on a fairly wide inlet, partly surrounded by the sea. This meant that the only means of transport to and from town was a traditional Italian gondola.

Coming back after an enjoyable evening meant that each boat was filled to capacity with men – mostly very merry men – who had been enjoying the local wines and spirits. This caused a certain amount of anxiety amongst those not so well 'lubricated'. . . We were quite anxious that the long narrow craft, which lay low in the water, could be easily upset by the boisterous passengers. The oarsman, however, standing high in the stern with his long-handled paddle and his oil lamp high in the very ornamental prow, slowly and rhythmically steered the boat and ignored the half drunken crowd, uttering not a word!

Early one morning, I stood at the entrance to my tent, enjoying the fresh sea breeze. The camp was still in its deep repose as there was no official reveille time. I observed a figure slowly sauntering down the row of tents, and as he got closer, I suddenly recognised a Wing Commander Padre, the one who had 'thrown away his dog collar' during the riotous night of the 'Great Binge' on the ward at Bari. He turned and looked in my direction, and then his voice rang out quite gleefully:

'Harry!! What a wonderful surprise!!'

After exchanging greetings, he suddenly asked, 'Have you ever been up to Rome?'

'Yes', I replied. 'I spent a 48-hour trip their last January, visiting virtually every inch of St Peter's, but we had very heavy snow storms, so I spent most of the time exploring the interior.'

'So . . .' he quizzed, 'You haven't been back again then?'

I replied in the negative.

'Right-oh, I have an idea', he replied conspiratorially and with a wide grin. 'I am proposing to send you on a special course, and you will be away for almost three months. It's a course on Art and Archaeology in Rome, something I thought that you would enjoy. You will be notified officially in due course. I'll have a word with Doc and find someone to replace you whilst you are away. Would you like to attend?'

I replied with an excited 'Yes please!!'

'I thought you would.' He smiled.

You can imagine my surprise and delight at this wonderful invitation!

✚

Rome

And so it was that for three months, soon after the cessation of hostilities in Europe – June, July and August 1945 – that I attended the 'Art, Archaeology and Moral Leadership' course in Rome, sponsored and organised by the British Government.

The students on this course numbered some sixty men and two women (one of whom was Sister, later Dame, Veronica Ashworth, whom I knew from 31 MFH), of all ranks and ages.

We were given full accommodation in the very spacious and well-appointed first class hotel 'Albergo Impero' on the Via Viminale. (*Interestingly, this hotel has survived the last eighty-plus years and still stands, much as Scra would have seen it when he was there.*)

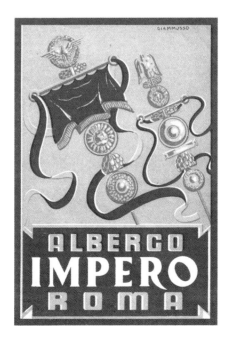

After arrival and dinner, we were given our instructions. We were told that it was an important course, and upon completion there would be an examination on both the contents of the course and the historical sites we were to visit. We then settled into our rooms. I was sharing a twin room with a new-found friend, and I must admit I slept like a log.

It was a fine bright morning when I awoke. The golden shafts of the early morning sun were filtering through the delicate lace curtains. I slowly arose from the luxury of a feather bed and its gleaming white sheets with some reluctance. Looking around properly in the morning light, I found the room to be fully carpeted and very tastefully furnished. In the other bed my new companion still slept soundly. My eyes strayed around the room absorbing every detail, from the immaculate bathroom with its coloured tiles and shower to the pictures on the walls and the soft carpet underfoot throughout the room. This was luxury of a kind that I wasn't used to after sleeping rough between a couple of blankets.

I looked out upon the quiet street and noticed two women dressed in black answering the summons of the tiny nearby church for mass. A tabby cat was vigorously washing itself; stretching its legs as it got up, it stole silently into the nearest house for its first meal of the day.

The air became filled with the ringing of innumerable bells from numberless churches around the city, summoning all for the first mass of the day. The time was 0600 hrs, an alarm call to arouse Rome's visitors from their deep sleep.

In the mornings we attended lectures given by eminent professors of history sent out from England, and then each day after lunch in the spacious restaurant of the hotel we were arranged in groups to be taken in specially adapted army lorries with newly installed wooden seating to visit the historical sites mentioned in the lectures by the tutors that morning.

Arriving back at the hotel around 1700 hrs local time allowed us time for a wash and brush-up before dinner at 1800 hrs, after which there was a question and answer session in the spacious ballroom for our group which finished at around 2200 hrs.

It would be simply impossible to describe in full detail the historical sites that we visited, such as the Colosseum, the ruined temples and of course St Peter's, which we toured from crypt to the ball beneath the

ROME

Course members' photo, Rome, June 1945.

cross on top of the Basilica. This could accommodate eight people, for an unsurpassed view of the 'Eternal City'.

We were ideally situated in almost the centre of Rome, and the nearest attraction was the huge Amphitheatre. This was the first site on our course, and the professor went into minute detail on the spot, giving us so much history that it was difficult to absorb each and every detail.

ROME

I found myself moving my feet backwards and forwards over the original stone slabs of one of the many extant tiers of seating, thinking of what had been seen from here for so many years.

Towards the end of the course, I was astonished and privileged to receive a summons to a private audience with the Pope himself, Pope Pius XII. As I have mentioned earlier I am a Protestant, a member of the Church of England, and not a Roman Catholic, so this was indeed an honour.

Having learned of my medical mission to Yugoslavia, the Pope wished to hear of the conditions of his children out there, and whether adequate supplies such as food and clothing were reaching them. I was happy to inform His Holiness that supplies of all kinds had been dropped by the RAF and that they had reached his children.

After spending an hour answering his searching and intelligent questions, he remarked, 'Is there anything that you wish me to bless, my son?'

'Yes, Holy Father, my wife gave me this ring as a keepsake before I came overseas. Would you please bless this?'

This he duly did.

Malta

After I finished the course I returned to 73 Sqn and to their new home in Malta.

We left Brindisi on a merchant ship, and during the voyage conditions were generally good. Now the war in Europe was over, there was no need for an escort or convoy.

The journey took about two days before we sailed into Valletta Grand Harbour. I slept rather comfortably for the one night in a hammock.

We stood on deck in the early morning sunshine watching the small island slowly becoming larger and clearer in the dazzling summer sunshine. It had been a pleasant trip, and the squadron were the only passengers – the pilots had flown their kites over the day we sailed, to the Air Force base at Halfar, which lay a mile or so from the capital, Valletta.

As we approached it, the island looked like a sandy-coloured lump sticking out of a rich, blue, calm sea. Not a vestige of pasture or trees could be seen. By this time the sun was climbing into the sky and the temperature rose with speed accordingly. Although we were accustomed to such heat, we endeavoured to find some shade on the ship before we landed.

As the medical branch, we occupied a spacious villa, within easy reach of one of the main aerodromes, so you can imagine, that the morning 'sick parades' there were well and truly patronised!

All personnel working in the sick bay were entitled to one full day off per week, which enabled you to get right away from routine and spend the day in Valletta.

Normally, before going off duty, a last minute check was made to ensure that efficiency was maintained during one's absence. My particular duty was concerned with the operating theatre, which was fully equipped and ready to deal with any emergency. Therefore all the

Street scene, Valetta.

instruments and dressings, etc. had to be in a sterile condition, and it was essential to brief the person who was to replace you.

On this particular occasion I was most insistent that I expected to find the theatre in exactly the same condition upon my return the next day; and if a case had been bought in and the theatre used, it was imperative that it should be cleaned and made sterile again. In addition, an entry should be made in the record case book of the treatment given.

I went on to spend a very enjoyable day in town, shopping. What surprised me though, after being in Italy, and especially in North Africa, was that the street vendors in Malta had Fry's chocolates in the little trays that they carried. In Malta you could buy anything, whereas in England I knew that everything was in short supply or rationed, most especially sweets and chocolates.

That day, I also had a good lunch and went to the cinema in the evening, returning to my quarters just before midnight. The next morning, I went on duty at 0800 as usual. Have you ever entered a room and felt that something was amiss but could not quite put your finger upon it? The theatre looked exactly as I had left it, but as I looked round, my eyes fell upon the records and case book. There was one entry: 'Case . . . throat examination', signed by the doctor.

So when my stand-in reported for duty, I naturally remarked upon his easy day, with only one case and that of low importance.

'Important?? Blimey!'

His face changed

'If you were here you would have gone through the roof!' he exclaimed

Let me first acquaint you with the procedure for reporting sick at this particular station. It was laid down, in general station orders, that no airman would be able to get his boots changed (ill-fitting, damaged, worn out, etc.) unless he had the Medical Officer's permission and had received a 'chit' (an official piece of paper from a superior officer) duly signed. He could only then apply to the Quartermaster (head of stores – 'This place is for storing things. If it were for issuing kit, it would be called "Issues" and not "Stores" . . .') for a new pair. The reasoning behind this was to avoid any 'frivolous' requests.

Sick parade was held at 0800 every day except Sunday, and when anyone wished to report sick, they first had to report to the unit Orderly

Room. The sufferers would then marched over to sick bay by the Orderly Sergeant of the day. A list, comprising the name, rank and number of all on the parade, was compiled by the said Sergeant and would then be handed in to the sick bay clerk.

> *Now, this may sound rather archaic even for the 1940s, but when I was a young soldier in a regular Army battalion, not only did you have to report sick, you had to do in your best parade uniform with highly polished boots, and carrying your overnight kit in case you were 'bedded down', i.e. admitted. This was not really conducive for any 'real illnesses', and I remember having to do this when I could hardly walk, let alone march, on the day I was admitted into hospital (another story of military madness . . .), where I spent the next YEAR with a very rare syndrome known as Atoxic Epidermal Necrolysis (Stevens-Johnson Syndrome)! This was in the late 1980s . . . It was the beginning of my story of becoming a Registered Nurse myself.*

It appears that on the morning of my absence, a young airman quite small in stature wanted his boots exchanged. It was rather a heavy sick parade of around thirty individuals. Eventually, his name was called to go in and see the doctor, and he was ushered into the 'inner sanctum', where he presented himself to the Duty Doctor.

'Well . . . what do you want?' enquired the MO

'It's me boots, sir . . .' came the timid reply

'What did you say'

'It's me boots.'

'Do you always speak like that? Have you always been husky?'

'No, sir.'

'Wait outside, I'll see you later'

This poor supplicant then resumed his seat in the waiting area, to await the doctor's pleasure.

At 1130, sick parade was over. The MO enjoyed a nice cup of tea, then started to make his way to the Officers' Mess for lunch. Upon opening his door, he spotted the young airman sitting meekly in the corridor, still holding his boots.

MALTA

'Ah yes . . . I'd forgotten about you. Come in, take your shoes off and get yourself onto the operating table.'

After a number of protestations the airman adopted a recumbent position on 'the slab', enabling the MO to examine his throat with a tongue depressor.

'There's nothing wrong here', he sniffed

To which the now very meek airman replied, 'It's me boots, sir.'

My replacement was right; I would have hit the roof. The entire process was bordering on farcical.

I spent most of the rest of my time in Malta continuing to paint in my spare time and even presenting my work at some service art shows. Nothing else of note took place in the sick bay.

The Sick Quarters staff at Halfar in Malta. Scra is in the middle, and third right is Sqdn/Ldr Bradley, the Senior Medical Officer. Second right is Corporal Wilson, about whom Scra asserts the following: 'Cpl Wilson parachuted into Yugoslavia, but almost immediately made for the coast, and was picked up by a British Gunboat. He was arrested upon arrival at Bari by Military Police, but was subsequently awarded the British Empire Medal (BEM)... for a mission not completed!'

Home at Last

Towards the end of 1945, I was informed that I was to be 'demobbed' in the New Year. Relief at last, but I was sad that I had learnt and endured so much over past three years that I would be unable to put into practice again. Medical work was something I enjoyed, but I had my old job, and my dear wife, waiting for me back in London.

So, just after Christmas, I sailed away from Malta on the first leg of the journey home. We docked at Marseille, and I boarded an old German train which had no windows and no light and was already partly full. There was only one lavatory per coach, and these were out of use at night!

Men were packed into these coaches, with some sleeping in the corridors and even in the lavatories themselves. Being fairly short – five feet three inches – I stayed and slept on a luggage rack all the way up through France.

We did stop occasionally at the places noted here, and in the illustrations from the book *The Way Back*, which was probably a play on title of the propaganda film 'The Way Ahead' with David Niven.

> Perpignan
> Toulouse
> Breve
> Limoge
> Chateauroux
> Paris
> And finally, Dieppe.

We were then put on a ferry across to Newhaven, where I boarded another train to my demob centre at RAF Hednesford, which lay some eight miles outside Stafford.

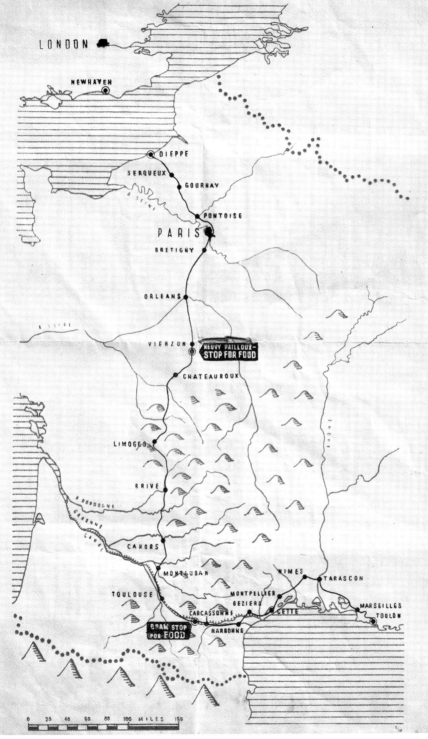

My final day in the RAF was 20th February 1946, whereupon I went home and now bring my story to an end.

> *When Harold retired, he and Marjorie moved down to West Sussex – on the border with East Sussex – where they lived in a small bungalow in the village of Keymer, surrounded by the roses which Scra tended himself.*
>
> *Sadly, Marjorie died in 1981, and Harry followed her in 1991. They are buried in the churchyard of St Cosmas and St Damien in Keymer.*

This book is dedicated to them, and to the now anonymous lady who saw fit to honour Scra's wish that his story be told and published and chose me to do it for him.

Per Ardua ad Astra

Further Reading and Bibliography

Bailey, Hamilton (ed.), *Surgery of Modern Warfare* (E&S Livingstone, Edinburgh, 1941)

Bloch, Herbert, *The Bombardment of Monte Cassino* (publisher unknown, 1979)

Butler, James (ed.), *History of the Second World War: The Mediterranean and Middle East, Vol V* (HMSO, London, 1973)

Clarke, Rupert, *With Alex at War* (Pen & Sword/Leo Cooper, Barnsley, 2000)

Ellis, John, *Cassino: the Hollow Victory* (André Deutsch, London, 1984)

Foot, M.R.D., *An Outline of the Special Operations Executive 1940 – 1946* (Random House, London, 1999)

Ford, Ken, *Cassino: The Four Battles, January– May 1944* (Crowood Press. Marlborough, 2001)

Hurst, Arthur, *Medical Diseases of War*, 3rd edition (Edward Arnold & Co, London, 1943)

Jolly, Douglas W., *Field Surgery in Total War* (Hamish Hamilton medical books, London, 1941)

McConville, Michael, *A Small War in the Balkans: British Military Involvement in Wartime Yugoslavia, 1941 – 1945* (Macmillan, London, 1986)

Majdalany, Fred, *Cassino: Portrait of a Battle* (Longmans, Green & Co, London, 1957)

Parker, Matthew, *Monte Cassino* (Headline, London, 2003)

Quarrie, Bruce. *German Paratroopers in the Med* (PSL, Cambridge, 1979)

Rexford-Welch, S.C. (ed.), *Medical History of the Second World War. The Royal Air Force Medical Services* (three volumes, HMSO, London, 1955)

Rogers, Lindsay, *Guerilla Surgeon* (Collins, London, 1957)

Vittiglio, Fred and Fiorill, Fernando, *Cassino – Bombe, Malaria e. Coraggio*, (Ciarrapico Editore, Rome, 1979)

Whiting, Charles, *Hunters from the Sky* (Leo Cooper/Purnell, London, 1975)

Whicker, Alan, *Whicker's War* (Harper Collins, London, 2005)

Index

11th Hussars, 9
1st Army, 9
281 Wing, 136, 167
43 Sqn, 149
50th British General Hospital, 130
73 Sqn, vi, 78, 106, 107, 110–11, 113–14, 117, 124, 133, 152, 157, 160, 171
7th Armd Div, 9
8th Army, 80

Ada (Scrafield), x
Adriatic, 73, 80, 107
Aeneas, 13
Africa, xii, 6, 7, 9, 13, 27, 48, 55, 60, 78, 133–4, 149, 173
Ahab, 54
Air Ambulance, 92
Albergo Impero Hotel, 163
Alexander, Field Marshal Harold, 125–7, 159
Algeria, 5
Algiers, 6–7, 46, 65, 72
Amphitheatre, 11, 31, 34, 67, 76, 166
Ancona, 156–7
Archaeology, 41, 162–3

Ariano, 78, 80
Ashworth, Dame Veronica, 41, 163
Atlas Mountains, 6
Austro-Hungarian Empire, 86

Balkan Air Force, 80, 87, 103
Balkans, 80, 86–7, 103, 157
Bari, 77–83, 86, 89, 136, 160, 162
Barletta, 79
Base Hospital, 89, 101, 109, 129
Batman, 58
Ben Masour, 7
Bihac, 103
Bizerte, 72
Bor-Kornime, 33
Bos, 103
Brindisi, 157, 160–1, 171
British Medical Mission, 87
Bully Beef, 140
Byrsa Hill, 11, 13, 17
Byrsa-Bougie, 28

Campobasso, 158
Canaan, 55
Cannae, 106–7, 113, 122, 133–5, 152, 157
Caravan, 107

Carpet making, 43–4
Carthage, vii, 6, 11–13, 24–30, 42–3, 54–5, 57, 59, 66, 69, 72, 82
Casbah, 29, 48, 52
Caserta Benevento, 78
Cathedral, 12–13, 15, 23, 59
Chetniks, 86
Christmas, 59–60, 65, 176
Churchill, Winston, 34, 126, 131
Cinema, 29, 173
Clark, General Mark, 126–8
Clark, Rupert, 103
Colosseum, 67, 164
Concentration camp, 103
Concert, 15, 17, 60
Convent, 12–13, 16, 32–3, 42–3, 54, 59, 71,
Convoy, 5–6, 59, 72–4, 77–8, 105, 135, 171
Courts Martial, 84, 121, 157
Coward, Noel, 161
Crimea, 139–40
Croats, 86, 102, 137
CWGC, 65, 151

Dakota, 104
Demob, 176
Dench, Flt/Lt FC, 86
Desert Rat, 53, 57
Dido, Queen, 12
Dinnick, Wing/Com Oswald Peter, 23, 65–6
Duchen, Lt Michael, 149, 152
Dunkirk, 128

East Grinstead, 102
Edinburgh, 40

El Djem, 67
El Harrach, 5
El Jem, 66
El-Allo-Ena, 9
Elijah, 54
ENSA, 161
Erk, 107
Ernest (Scrafield), x
Eternal City, 13
Examination, 1, 2, 24, 30, 164, 173

Fallschirmjäger, 121
Florence, 139–40
Foggia, 157

Galilee, 55
General Hospital, 2, 37, 130
George Medal, 113, 152
Geraldo, 161
Gillies, Sir Harold, 102
Good Friday, 46
Gospels, 54
Gradiska, 103
Gramophone, 55
Greece, 80, 134
Ground Staff, 65, 136
Guinea Pigs, 102
Gustav Line, 120

Halfar, 171
Hammamet, 43–5, 47–8
Hannibal, 7, 12–13, 107
Harding, General John, 126
Harrup, George, 23
Highbury, 10
Himmler, Heinrich, 87
Holy See, 127

INDEX

Horrocks, General Brian, 7
Hotel de Golf, 44
Hovender, 10
Hutton, 10–11

Italy, viii, xii, 13, 141, 72–3, 79–80, 103, 107, 112, 126–8, 132, 135, 152, 156–7, 173

Jaundice, 57, 68–9
Jerboa, 53, 57–8
Jesonovac Concentration Camp, 103
Joan (Scrafield), 11
Jolley, Major Douglas, 16

Kairouan, 47–8, 54–5, 57, 59
Kasserine Pass, 66
Kesselring, Field Marshal Albert, 7, 126
Keymer, Sussex, 178
Khaki drill, 5
Kingdom of Yugoslavia, 86
Krieglazerett, 17

LCT, 136–7, 155
Le-Khroub, 7, 9
Limehouse, x
London, x, 15, 21, 41, 55, 66, 124, 139, 158, 176
Ludo, 121, 124
Luftwaffe, 121

M & B Tabs, 131, 140
Maclean, Brig. Sir Fitzroy, 87
Madjez-El-Bab, 7
Maison Carré, 6, 46

Maison Lavigerie, 12–13, 16, 68
Malta, xii, 135, 171, 173, 175
Mantovani, 161
Marjorie (Scrafield), x, xii, 178
MASH, 16
Matron, 2, 41–2, 130
May and Baker, Dagenham, 131
McCabe, Jim, LAC, GM, 113, 115
McGrath, Flt/Lt 'Doc', 110
McIndoe, Sir Archibald, 102
Mediterranean, 13, 32, 72, 151
Merlin, 114
Messina, 72
Mihajlovic, Draza, 86
Mission Rogers, 87
Mobile Field Hospital, v, 16, 22, 41–2
Monks (White Fathers), 59
Monte Cassino, 116–17, 126
Moscow, 86
Mosque, 36
Mother Superior, 18, 42
Mustang, 148

NAAFI, 18, 78, 105, 161
Naples, 52, 73–4, 78, 127
Nightingale, Florence, 137, 139–40
Niven, David, 176
Nova Gradiska, 103
Nuns, 12, 18–19, 42–3
Nursing Orderly, vii, viii, 112, 132

Old Testament, 54
Operation Bingham, 136
Operation Capri, 7
Operation Typical, 87

Padre, 85, 162
Pag, 136
Palermo, 72
Partisan, 80, 86–8, 101, 103, 136–7, 151, 154–5, 157
Peaty, LAC Driver Bob, 114, 129–30, 134
Penicillin, 130–1
Peretola Airfield, Florence, 151
Phoenicians, 11
Piraeus, 134
Plastic Surgery, 102
PMRAFNS, 41–2
Pneumonia, 131–2
Pompeii, 30, 74
Pope Pius XII, 170
Portici, 73
Post Mortem, 65–6
Poultice, 131–2
Prison, 21
Probus, 27
Propaganda, 10, 176
Punic, 13, 24

QAIMNS, 42
Queen Victoria Hospital, 102

RAF, vii, viii, xii, 66, 15–18, 41–2, 52, 58, 84, 87, 102, 107, 113–14, 136, 156–8, 170, 176, 178
RAF Police, 52, 113
RAF Regiment, 52
RAMC, 16
Refugees, 89–104
Reichstag, 128
Road Accident, 46

Rogers, Major Lindsay, 87–8, 157
Roman Circus, 67
Roman Hall of Justice, 30, 32–3
Romany, 87
Rome, 13, 41, 120, 126–7, 162–4, 166
Rommel, Field Marshal Erwin, 7
Royal Navy, 136

Sandhurst (RMA), 86
Sanski Most, 103
Scipio, 12
Scrafield, vii, x, xi, xii
Serbs, 86–7
Setif, 7
Shrapnel, Lt John, 38
Sicily, 71
Sick bay, 108, 116, 171, 174–5
Sidi-Boo-Said, 27
Sidmouth, 3–4
Sister A, 39–41
Sister B, 39–41
Slovenes, 86
SOE, vii, 86–7, 157
Souk Ahras, 7
South Africa, 126, 148–9, 151
South African War Graves Project, 151
Soyer Stove, 89, 139–40
Soyer, Alexis, 138, 140
Spitfire, 78–9, 107, 113–14, 116
SS, 87
St Peter's (Rome), 162, 164
Stalingrad, 120
'Stand-by Drome Duty', 59, 116
Stoke Newington, x

INDEX

Stromboli, 73
Suicide, 60
Surgeons, 16, 46, 56, 59, 65–6, 68, 87, 157
Sussex, vii, xi, 102, 178

Tanit, 24, 27
Tanith, 24
Temple of Venus, 17
Tented Hospital, 46, 52, 54–5, 57, 59
Termoli, 78
Texas Transit Camp, 72
Tito, Marshal Josef, 86–7, 103, 137, 154
Torre Annunziata, 73
Troy, 13
Tuberculosis, Pulmonary, 92
Tunis, 5–10, 12, 17, 21, 24, 28, 36, 41, 48, 52, 59, 66
Tunisia, 6–7, 15, 29, 72
Typhoid, 43
Typhus suits, 92
Tyrrhenian Sea, 73

U-Boats, 9, 72
Ultra Code, 9
Ustase, 86–7

Valetta, 172
Vermouth, 28, 78, 121, 157
Vesuvius, 74, 76
Virgil, 12
Volcano, 73, 76

Walworth, 21, 22
Wandsworth, 11
Wellington bomber, 113
Whicker, Alan, 127
White Sisters, vii, 12–13, 17–18, 43
William Edward Scrafield, x
Williams, LAC L, 113
Winter Line, 119
Woking, x
Wounded, 17–18, 59, 88, 130, 139

Yugoslavia, vii, 12, 80, 86, 103, 106, 136, 151–2, 157, 170

Zada, 136
Zara, 136